No Mistake

The Science of Money, a Great Truth

Gold Legal Tender, Bills of Exchange, Exports and Imports, Balance....

No Mistake

The Science of Money, a Great Truth
Gold Legal Tender, Bills of Exchange, Exports and Imports, Balance....

ISBN/EAN: 9783337111960

Printed in Europe, USA, Canada, Australia, Japan

Cover: Foto ©Suzi / pixelio.de

More available books at **www.hansebooks.com**

From the HON. HORACE GREELEY.

NEW YORK, May 5, 1870.

DEAR SIR:

I have yours of the 27th ult.

I think you have struck upon a great truth—or at least a corner of it. I am not sure that your plan has all the elements of success—am quite confident it has some of them. Let us study and ponder until the whole truth shall be clearly manifest.

Yours,

HORACE GREELEY.

W. B. PARTEE, ESQ.

THE SCIENCE OF MONEY

A GREAT TRUTH.

GOLD LEGAL TENDER, BILLS OF EXCHANGE, EXPORTS AND IMPORTS, BALANCE OF TRADE, FAVORABLE OR UNFAVORABLE BALANCE OF EXCHANGE.

ALL SIMPLIFIED AND MADE CLEARLY MANIFEST.

BY

NOMISTAKE.

PHILADELPHIA:
J. B. LIPPINCOTT & CO.
1871.

Entered according to Act of Congress, in the year 1870, by

J. B. LIPPINCOTT & CO.,

In the Office of the Librarian of Congress at Washington.

TO

THE MEMORY OF THE LATE

JAMES DICK,

THE PRINCE OF NEW ORLEANS MERCHANTS,

WHOSE HONOR AND INTEGRITY

GAVE HIM FRIENDS IN THE HOUR OF NEED,

ENABLING HIM TO SAVE FROM THE DISASTERS OF 1837

AN HONORABLE NAME,

AND THE MEANS OF DOING MUCH GOOD

TO FRIENDS AND RELATIONS,

This humble Work,

OF ONE WHO SHARED HIS GAINS

AND ENDEAVORED TO PROFIT BY HIS COUNSELS,

IS RESPECTFULLY DEDICATED

BY

THE AUTHOR.

INTRODUCTION.

In offering the following reflections deduced from observations on the circulating medium and exchanges of our country, together with the central idea of a divorcement of money of account from all articles of merchandise, I am well aware of the opposition I will have to encounter from the long-standing prejudices in favor of gold as a legal tender and circulating medium. I only ask a patient and thoughtful perusal of my arguments, assuring the reader that in pointing out a sure road to the liquidation of our large and onerous debt, I do not offer it as a clap-trap to gain advocates. The whole is only secondary to the inauguration of a permanent legal tender which will not be an article of merchandise.

I did not undertake this investigation with any reference to our national debt, but solely with the hope of giving to the country a cheaper medium in effecting her internal exchanges. The subject is so fruitful of thought, leading one, as it were, through all the field of political economy, that I deem it advisable, in the present agitated state of our finances, to pursue it in connection with the liquidation of our debt, especially as no opportunity could be more favorable for the demonstration of the principle I have undertaken to set up.

To insure the establishment of a great principle, it must be brought forward at the proper time, when the thoughts and feelings as well as interest of all parties can be called into play.

This is at present the situation of the United States. She has a legal tender and circulating medium of her own, but still lives in adultery with gold; and I advocate a divorce, that the future offspring may be legitimate.

In advocating so great a change I am fully aware "that there surely must be some foundation for opinions so generally embraced by mankind, and that we ourselves ought rather to call in question the observations and reasonings which overturn what has been hitherto so uniformly maintained and acquiesced in by so many individuals, distinguished alike by their wisdom and benevolence."

The profound investigations of Lardner retarded, but did not arrest, ocean steam navigation; skepticism did not deter Morse from giving to the world the telegraph; nor did Washington falter to give us a republic, when all past history condemned the experiment. It is the hope that co-operation will bring success to this divorcement that leads me now to lay it before the country. As I do not promise to put money in any man's pocket, otherwise than by industry and economy, I trust I shall not be condemned as selfish or visionary, but shall be regarded as making an honest effort to accomplish good.

The following are the points I have endeavored to establish:

If the legal tender and circulating medium of a country be at times desirable for export, it will become a curse to the people instead of a blessing.

Production in excess of consumption will alone enable a people to pay taxes.

No country can have credit long without surplus productions, this being the basis of all national credit.

No country has ever offered her capital stock in payment of debt. To do so, if it were held by a foreign power, would be to surrender nationality.

Money has no other use than to buy with or to liquidate debt.

Between countries money loses its value as money from its peculiar character, and is only received as a commodity in exchange.

It is not the export or import of any one article that impoverishes a nation or replenishes its wealth. It is the difference in gain or loss by the exchange.

Productions command productions; the medium to effect the exchange is conventional, and may have no other value.

The merchant creates the demand, without which production for sale must cease.

The incentive to production is consumption or to sell, the object of which is to buy and gratify desires.

There would be no selling if it did not give ability to buy. Selling enables you to buy, and stimulates production.

Digestion limits the desire for food; luxuries have

no bounds. Capital cannot be used in the former beyond gratification; in the latter it has no limits.

If all men were misers, there would be no production.

All produce gravitates to the point where it is most in demand, and that point is where there is greatest ability to buy.

Merchants cannot become opulent if production is but little over consumption.

Gold is not the circulating medium between countries,—it is bills of exchange; and gold becomes merchandise.

A full investigation of this subject is invited, and I beg that all strictures and criticisms be forwarded to me at Vicksburg, Mississippi.

NOMISTAKE.

CONTENTS.

	PAGE
Gold Legal Tender	13
Fluctuations—their Effect	43
Bills of Exchange—Modern Use	57
Balance of Trade	64
Application	66
Consolation	70
Legal Tender	71
Who pays the Expense and Charges of a Medium	74
Instinct	82
Gold Legal Tender and Circulating Medium	85
Legal Tender	97
Divorcement of Gold from Circulating Medium	100
Production and Consumption	104
Credit through Circulating Notes	114
Medium should be Legal Tender	117
Legal Tender only to be issued for Bonds	129
Trial and Summary	134
Production and its Drawbacks	145
Circulating Medium and Legal Tender	149
Production and Circulating Medium	155
Circulating Medium a Necessity	157
Legal Tender, Balance of Trade, Cotton Crop, etc.	160
"Favorable or Unfavorable Balance of Exchange"—What it means	171
Legal-Tender Circulating Notes not made Legal Tender, a Curse to Production	176
Debt, Interest, and Legal Tender	181
Medium of Exchange	187
Exchange and Medium	198
True Basis of all Mediums	202
Deductions	212

SCIENCE OF MONEY.

GOLD LEGAL TENDER.

The currency of a country, based on land or property as a measure of value, will depreciate the moment the income or annual rent falls short of the average of production. But if income be its basis, and likewise be the measure of value, the depreciation can never be so great as to absorb all value; it is this error in the issue of an inconvertible currency or medium of exchange that produces all the losses and troubles to individuals or a government. Consequently it is quite different if the income be fixed and certain; but allow any other standard to measure the value of property or its availability, and you subject it to the whims of the speculators or the demands of the fortunate holders of the standard or measure of value. This error in estimates or foundation of value cannot but be temporary if based on annual income, this being a reserve over immediate consumption; if we confine our estimates to income or production alone, many fluctuations will be avoided.

The medium of exchange, or the circulating medium, of a country, has no effect or value in the exchange between countries; the supply, of whatever it may be, adjusts itself to the demand, and leaves the trade or exchanges of the two countries precisely in the same condition as if they were bartering one commodity for the other. An increase or diminution of the medium of exchange in any one of the countries affects only itself, and not the exchangeable value of the commodities the one country desires to barter with the other: hence the conclusion which cannot be altered by the quantity of the medium. The result, after all, is but the exchange or barter of the one surplus for the other. He who has the power to buy or a surplus to exchange is in a better condition than the party who has no surplus; the former can supply all his wants, the latter must be pinched and restricted, and may complain of hard times. The one who has not the wherewithal to supply his wants will forever remain in the same condition and be complaining. The depreciation of a currency does not affect the foreign trade or have any influence over the demand and supply, each retaining its relative value in exchange.

The change of a circulating medium affects value only at the beginning and the end. The United States has destroyed all the values in her power by the change, and it now remains to be seen in what way she may continue the existence of legal tenders. If the government be prudent, wise, and economical in the future, and shall never at any time allow issuance, or force others on the market, except in exchange for bonds, the legal tenders must continue to carry the same value of a four per cent. gold-bearing bond. The fluctuations from this center can only be such as are incident to supply and demand, the excess or shortness being only to the extent of a temptation being offered in rates of interest to cause the conversion of bonds into legal tenders, and *vice versa*.

We will suppose a case or position of trade where the legal tender, as a circulating medium, is not equal to its wants, and no one in the country has bonds to convert and supply the deficiency. Immediately the price of bonds would rise in the market, and cause their importation, like any other commodity or value in exchange for any surplus production we may have. This will continue until an equilibrium or equation of supply and demand is established. Even should the premium paid seem excessive, the circulating medium must and will be supplied so long as there remains in the country a surplus of value from which speculators can hope to gain a profit from their exchange; and when this state of the market does occur,—and sooner or later it will,—then legal tenders may claim a premium over gold or at par. This, in commercial parlance, is a resumption of specie payment. When it does come thus, it is more likely to continue than when brought about by financial arrangement or temporary expedient.

There need be no fears in regard to a supply of gold, as all commodities tend to the most profitable market, and that market will be found where there is the greatest abundance of produce to sell or exchange. Those who have the ability to buy can always supply their wants.

It is certainly an object with any country having a specie circulating medium to desire as large a sum as possible for her exports to be returned in coin; hence the general anxiety of all parties to see a constant stream of bullion flowing into their country. This is natural, as the tendency is to cheapen money and advance the price or value of all other commodities. They do not consider that they have gained nothing in wealth, but have only changed the relative value or exchangeable value of commodities. It may be they have exchanged an article much needed for reproduction for one that is of no value until exchanged for something else. It is but the hoarding of a value that could have been made profitable; consequently, so long as it remains idle, the income, to the full extent of the average profits of the country, is lost, not only to the individual, but to the country, and the inference is that the country exchanging the gold has realized the profit due to the producer.

The prosperity of a country depends more on moderate profits and uniform prices than on the extreme fluctuations incident to speculation. The latter tend to discourage production and industry—the majority of producers favoring the occupation least fluctuating. The prudent, plodding class desire that the money rate of interest should indicate the rate of profit, instead of the embarrassment growing out of extreme speculation, when the current interest demanded for the use of capital in productive enterprise is the measure of profit realized. No great losses can flow from the lending or borrowing of it, if limited to time in the permanency of the investment. It is the sudden fluctuations either in interest or of production that tend to discourage reproduction from the annual accumulation of energy and economy.

In the divorcement of the circulating medium of a country from all articles of merchandise in which foreign trade can participate, you have at once confined the fluctuations to the home demand, and it is but reasonable to credit the producer with ability to measure his own wants, and to assume that he will, in parting with his surplus, demand in exchange just such goods, wares, and gold as may be most suitable to his future desires. The agriculturists of a country are not so conversant with the supplies of other markets as are the merchants and traders,— hence the farmer will advise with the trader as to the time and place for effecting the exchange, but not as to the particular articles needed by him in the future. No one can tell what quantity of legal tenders, mess-pork, flour, or clothing is needed so well as the one whose surplus is to be exchanged for them.

However you may arrange, or even multiply and mix up, money with produce, after all, the former is but the medium by which the exchange is effected; the latter is the purchase, and the result is produce for produce. Now, this being universally the *modus operandi*, and considered as the end and purpose of production, why should I be required to value my property in comparison with a commodity influenced by all the speculations and complications of the world? And, after all, the result is only an exchange of mess-pork for flour,—the demand for gold to purchase tea in China, or for silver to be given for wines and silks of France. It matters not how much of the precious metal may be demanded for the speculation, the interior exchange of the country should not, and need not, be involved in the perturbations of so uncertain an agency.

When I go to market with my pork, I do not wish to be compelled to sell it for a commodity or medium that may be in France or China, but for one that is local, and which, I know, will be received for flour. This is what I call common sense and honesty, and the holding out to industry and enterprise the greatest inducements to increased production, for which they may hope for an equitable exchange.

The merchant finds me a market for my produce, and brings in exchange the surplus of others which I need. Neither of us can prosper without influencing the future of the other. The gambling speculator adds nothing to society in morals or wealth, but is ever plunging the producers and traders into misery and distress.

I do not claim for this local currency a complete immunity from fluctuations and occasional periods of embarrassment. No human institution is free from change or from foreign complications in effecting our internal exchanges with our local medium; that never can be secured if we continue the same measure of value in use as a circulating medium. Measure of value should be unchangeable, not arbitrary; we can fix measure of time and space, but not of value.

Man's nature will affix values to his own property in accordance with *fancy* or *interest*,—whether he will exchange his dog, estimated at one hundred dollars, for two fifty-dollar puppies, or for one; and if he should give his obligation on time for a gun, it is reasonable to suppose he will be as desirous afterwards to confine to the country the legal tenders for the one as that there will be game to hunt with his dog and gun. From his industry he expects to produce the flour or pork which will command on the spot the legal tenders to make good his maturing obligations. To sum up all in a word, I am in favor of all men issuing their obligations to be paid in any commodity they may select, even in puppies, if this obligation should be a legal tender, and the measure of them should be the payment of four per cent. interest per annum in gold. The fluctuations cannot long exceed the current rate of interest. And as these fluctuations in value only remotely influence the comparative value of produce, the sacrifice which may become necessary in meeting maturing obligations will be measured not by the present, but by the remote period of the maturing bond, which is the basis of the legal tender. If this legal tender were gold and not in the country, or near at hand, the loss would fall entirely on the present and not on the future.

However much others may desire the produce to be exchanged for the legal tender, it is but presenting two problems for solution, in the elucidation of one principle.

You might as well attempt to establish by law two

legal tenders, to remain, and at all times have equal value, as to presume to inaugurate a measure of value and a circulating medium to be one and the same. The two, from their nature and object, are incompatible. When one goes up, the other must go down. Both are intended to occupy the same bed,—but the one at night, the other during the day. Our own country for a long time endeavored to enforce two standards of value, gold and silver, but found the laws of trade such that no edict could force men to pay obligations otherwise than in the cheaper commodity, this remaining the legal tender, while the other became an article of traffic and export. The same result will, some day, be deemed not only practicable but advisable, in regard to fixing one legal tender and one measure of value. It is impossible to make the two one and the same, and still be just to those who desire only a medium of exchange, and to those also who wish to measure values. It is a well-known fact, that the transfer of the precious metals from one country to another will cause what is called cheap money in the one, and dear in the other, and that precisely in the ratio of that obstruction, in the one, more of an article of production must be given in exchange for the standard of value than formerly, in the other less will be demanded. This must go on until an equitable exchange of commodities and the precious metals is established, however disastrous it may be to the country in the mean time.

We can have no better illustration of the effect of a standard of value of gold or of legal tenders for the circulating medium than our own present imperfect standard as demonstrated a few weeks ago. The universal measure of value, gold, appreciated twenty-five per cent. when compared with legal tenders, and again depreciated twenty-five per cent., between breakfast and dinner.

Suppose you had had an obligation maturing on the day of this great gold bubble, and the measure of its value had been gold. Had you delayed payment until near the close of banking-hours, it would have cost you one-fourth of your estate to liquidate it. Now, is it not clear that this decline and advance had no relation to the value of the commodity which you received when the obligation was entered into, or to its present exchangeable value? It was the speculative influence so often brought to bear on an article of merchandise, and its disasters ended where they should end,—in the *gold rooms*. The only effect on the producer of the country was sympathetic, and it is to rid the country of this influence that I am laboring.

Take the reverse of this gold obligation, say that your maturing obligation was payable in legal tenders, for which you were called on that day, the enhanced value of these legal tenders could only have been the fluctuation in the market value of the bond on which they were raised, and this could be estimated only by the difference of interest on the advance or decline in the standard or measure of value, and not on the whole amount. In the former case you would have become bankrupt,—in the latter you could have honorably discharged your obligation with slight loss to yourself and none to your country.

Many will contend that if the circulating medium be other than the precious metals, it will sooner or later drive all the gold out of the country. The very admission of this is but an argument in favor of a cheaper medium, it being unreasonable to suppose that individuals will send off or exchange their gold for trifles. So far from this, more often than otherwise it is exchanged for something for reproduction which can be turned to profitable account in the future.

From a predilection in favor of gold, men often part with values they should retain, but yield to the temptation and the hope of replacing those values on more favorable terms. A party sending off his gold to procure something to be placed in the line of reproduction, furnishes an evidence not only of thrift, but that he has substituted a cheaper medium by which to effect his internal exchanges. And if ever again he is in want of gold, the productions which he has in hand will command all he may desire. There can be no greater fallacy than the exploded idea that the exportation of gold is any more impoverishing to a country than the exchange of other commodities, many of which are deemed more valuable and absolutely essential to reproduction, such as food, clothing, etc. These cannot be dispensed with, and these alone can be relied on to command labor and forward the simplest enterprises.

To suppose that the people of a country will part

with their gold and not receive in return a substantial value, is to argue that they need a guardian, and the party desiring to direct them must have no interest in the exchange. There can be no safety in the counsels of one claiming the omnipotent power of a general administration of the private affairs of his country. One of the greatest difficulties attending a circulating medium not convertible into gold in times of depression and panic, is to know what to do with it in case of suspension. And it is this uncertainty that quickens the desire to convert, or, as it is now called, to realize. This state of uncertainty cannot attend United States legal tenders, as the privilege of conversion at will into a four per cent. annuity, or bond, payable in gold, gives to the holder this sure outlet.

So long as the government maintains good faith with her people and the holders of her funded and circulating debt, no sudden or great derangement or fluctuation can be entailed on the country generally. At most, such derangement can be but temporary, and as the entire country will have an interest in the recovery, united effort will cause the loss to be small.

The general confidence and disposition to uphold the standard are quite different from any local authority to issue circulating notes. The spirit of rivalry often does more than extreme want to embarrass and depress the operations of individuals.

Confidence and credit in commercial affairs, but more especially in banking, cover more than three-fourths of the transactions connected with the exchange of commodities; as an evidence, capital itself will disappear whenever confidence is withdrawn.

At this time, the two hemispheres are mourning the loss of one whose credit was equaled only by his charities while living. But a few years ago, this great philanthropist had to ask the Bank of England for the promise of temporary aid. No sooner was it promised than confidence was inspired, not only in his immense assets but also in the credits of all others in like situation. In banking or exchange-dealing, confidence is far more profitable than capital. Any exchange-dealer will tell you that with five hundred thousand dollars he will safely conduct a business of twenty million dollars, or forty to one. By confining the business to the capital, not more than one-tenth could be effected. This difference is due to the cheapening influence of credit; and to the full extent of this saving is the country furnished with the means of reproduction and extended profit. In all other commercial affairs, a business of only three, four, or five to one can be entered into and safely relied on.

For nearly ten years the country has effected its internal exchanges with an irredeemable, inconvertible legal-tender currency. No other ten years will show less fluctuation in production, or greater immunity from periodical embarrassment. The influx and efflux of gold have been constant, and equal to the wants of commerce. At no time has there been a dearth. During all this time the internal and external exchanges have been unprecedentedly large,—sustaining a tax-list equal to the entire exports of the country before the war. The harmony of all this is due to the partial divorcement of the internal exchanges from gold. Perfect this system, —make it perpetual and certain,—freeing the country from man-traps and spring-guns, in the shape of resumption and repudiation, and a degree of unexampled prosperity will crown our country's efforts,—efforts far surpassing the gigantic struggles of the past. To illustrate the effects of a medium of gold and one of legal tenders, suppose one dollar of gold to represent the measure of a day's work,—the equivalent of a certain amount of mess-pork, flour, etc. In order to carry on reproduction, I go to the capitalist, Mr. Gold, and borrow one hundred dollars, and use it in the production of cotton. In order to simplify, I leave out rates of interest, profit, etc. It is reasonable to suppose that the one hundred days' work will produce sufficient to relieve Mr. Gold from his advances. But when I go to the merchant with my cotton to be exchanged for gold, I am told by him that it is all in China, but that he has a friend, "an unconscionable dog," who will give him eighty dollars for the one hundred dollars in China. Being compelled to make my promise good, having no other alternative, I accept the offer. I return to Mr. Gold, and find myself twenty dollars short. Rather than sacrifice me by taking my mule and plow, he advises me to take one hundred and thirty dollars in legal tenders, which will command one hundred days' labor. I gladly accept the offer, and go into cotton again. When it is again ready for market, I return to the same merchant, and am informed that all the world has been sending gold to exchange for bills drawn against cotton, and that he will give me one hundred and thirty dollars in legal tenders and twenty dollars in gold for my cotton. This will enable me to make good my old and my new promise, and determine me in the future to make no promises of produce except such as I know can be raised in the country.

It is the accumulation of capital from past savings in a country which must be looked to for its development. This is contrary to the idea of many who oppose concentration, if in the hands of a few individuals; the reverse of which is true and the only safety. If capital were in the hands of the majority, or divided on the agrarian principle, all would be *shavers*. The large capitalist wants a certain interest, which he can and will diminish with the security. The shaver must have his pound of flesh, even if nearest the heart.

The capitalist may give tone to the market in quiet times, and furnish the Gazette with quotations, but in times of sharp competition, and derangement of supply and demand, the *middle-men* are always on the market, dictate terms, and furnish quotations. The capitalist who is accumulating, or, in every-day language, growing rich, is investing his earnings of rents and interest, silent and smooth in his course, like a deep stream. He is interested only in procuring a safe and profitable investment for his annual or semi-annual accumulation.

However small the rate of interest may be, he can

live and prosper, and is not influenced by anything but security. It is not so with the *middle-man*. He has borrowed at a rate and must lend at an advance, in order to realize a profit from which to draw his living. And thus it is as you descend in the scale of dealers in money—each drawing from it a living—the discount or premium widens, until you reach the shaver, who speculates on the necessities of mankind. The capitalist is aiding reproduction,—the shaver endeavoring to draw its fruits into his own pocket.

To illustrate: Mr. Snyder went to an eminent Virginia politician and *shaver* with a note having fourteen months to run. He inquired the rate of discount, and was told that it was so much per month. After the calculation was made, he was informed that the note *did not hold out*—in other words, the note did not equal the discount. This should be a warning to all young men, in their estimate of small losses. Give those small losses time and discount them at once, and presently will come the day of bankruptcy, or when the note will not hold out.

It is certainly the interest of the government and of its people that as large an amount as possible of its bonds and indebtedness be retained in the hands of its citizens.

Nothing will hold out a stronger inducement than to declare them representative of a legal tender. This will make all parties desirous of having at hand bonds, even if in small amount, in order that they may at any time convert them into legal tenders. If a horse or an ox be required, they know that payment can be promised without experiencing the doubts and uncertainties of converting any other portion of their stock into legal tenders.

I cannot illustrate better than by reference to the game of *faro*, in which you must have *counters*, in order to avoid the inconvenience of a subdivision of the money. Now, to get these counters you must go to the bank with something acceptable to the keeper. The substance required you may not have, and in order to obtain it you must sacrifice perhaps one or two assets. Now, if you knew the precise article that would procure these counters, it is but reasonable to suppose that you would keep some portion of your surplus invested in it. You know that it may be needed daily, or, at least, periodically.

The time will come when every prudent dealer or producer will have by his side a reasonable *reserve fund* of bonds with which he can at any time procure legal tenders by the abatement of interest for a certain time. Not so, however, if he must resort to an ordinary banking establishment. It may be that one or two days of his time is lost in dancing attendance on a board of directors. Even should he have the bonds to offer as security, he may fail to procure the accommodation or discount if the parties to whom he applies are engaged in the same line of speculation. They may promise fair, talk favorably up to the last moment, and then inform him that it can't be "*did.*"

If he has the United States bonds in his pocket, he can act like an independent man, without cringing to any clique, command the legal tenders and at once consummate his business. Now I beg leave to return to the other dealer of faro, who keeps the counters. When the producer returns to the market again, desiring some more counters to enable him to make a little operation, he finds that the faro-dealer left on the last steamer for Baden-Baden, having been advised by telegraph that a good thing could be made out of his counters there, on account of the small competition and large accumulation of values in that market. Many think that because gold is the circulating medium of the world, it is all the time used in that capacity. They do not remember that it ceases to be a medium or measure of value whenever it is in demand for export, and goes into the hands of those whose specialty is dealing in this commodity. A commodity it certainly has become, and is nothing more than so many barrels of mess-pork or bales of cotton collected at the point of export by the dealer.

The circulating medium between exports and imports being now bills of exchange, and no longer gold, or any other device to be used as counters or the medium of internal exchange, at this point I would call attention to one or two facts. You have seen the gold circulating medium collected by the dealer and exporter. What must be done for a medium to be used in return?

There are still productions to be bartered and exchanged in order that further production may go on and obligations be liquidated. Will you have the machinery of commerce stand still until the gold can be attracted by some great sacrifice of values? When it does come, as it will do if you have goods to offer at a bargain, it can answer no other purpose than to liquidate a debt between John Doe and Richard Roe, or to effect the exchange of mess-pork for flour.

Any other counter or legal tender would not have subjected consumption and production to all this delay. But how answer the same purpose? We could have awaited the return of the gold as merchandise in exchange for our cotton, provided we did not need calico instead. At any rate, the great end of production and consumption has been effected.

To demand of gold to act two distinct parts at the same time—as a medium of exchange and as merchandise in trade—is to attempt to endow it with omnipresence.

If two substances cannot be made to occupy the same space at the same time, two spaces cannot be filled at the same time by one and the same substance.

The honorable merchant must have the gold here the day his obligation matures, no matter what amount of other goods must be sacrificed. Those unworthy of credit will hold for *to-morrow*, however much they may sacrifice their neighbors. Bill Arp was not in the war himself, but he was willing to sacrifice all his relations in the cause.

The United States has now an independent circulating medium in her legal tenders, and as much gold as is equal to the wants of commerce, with a large reserve to meet her own maturing obligations.

The only incubus resting on trade and the circulating medium is the apprehension of a return to gold as a circulating medium. We have all we want as a measure of value,—productions measure productions. When gold was our circulating medium and measure of value, a few millions accumulated in the treasury caused such derangement that the government was compelled to divide it out among the States, in order to restore harmony. But now, with one hundred millions in the treasury, productions still command productions, however much our circulating medium may be appreciated or depreciated by comparison with gold.

In specie-paying times, to have hoarded up this amount of gold would have bankrupted the circulation of our country and deranged the equilibrium of trade in all parts of the commercial world.

We are using a circulating medium independent of all the world. From this channel gold has been withdrawn, and now occupies the same position as cotton, pork, and flour. So long as we have other articles of value to export, no one will call for gold. On the other hand, so long as we have a surplus to exchange for it, we will never be without that universal commodity. A country which has not bread, nor anything to exchange for it, must perish. Gold it can do without. Nor will a people trouble itself much about it so long as their productions can be turned into the productions of others which they require for consumption or reproduction. It is the increase in production which calls for an increase in the circulating medium. All sums above this demand are, to a certain extent, not needed,—thrown on the market, and, to that extent, worthless.

The use of a circulating medium, or the consent to have one, creates the measure for it. Hence the difference between commodities and the medium of exchange. Commodities demand a medium of exchange, but the medium demands nothing, and, if redundant, becomes worthless to that extent. A circulating medium is not used because of any intrinsic value, but it has been made the medium.

It has been recommended as being equal to the cure of this disease, and should not be looked upon as a universal *panacea*, and called a measure of value as well as a medium of exchange.

Steamboats are in their element when on navigable streams, locomotives when on the iron track; neither can assume the position of the other with safety or profit. Where is, or can be, the controversy in regard to the utility or necessity of a circulating medium to effect the exchanges of the country? Can there be any as to the gain of interest to the party having power to issue them? This point being conceded, no one certainly can be so selfish as to wish to deprive the people of what belongs to them by right and risk. If there is any prospect of loss, by all construction of law and justice, the party risking it should participate in the profits.

I am well aware that many will contend that if the assuming power of circulating notes should be solely in the hands of the government, the effect would be to close up all the private banking establishments against making discount. To a certain extent this may be the case, but it will only apply to the *wildcat* concerns that attempt to speculate on the credulity of the people, and at no time had any other capital than what the people deposited with them, whilst giving them credit and circulating a note, and paying, in the majority of cases, a shaving rate of discount, when the note is not as solvent as the one discounted, these notes frequently being rediscounted to create a fund for the speculative directors to gamble on, and when the collapse does come the solvent note of the producer must be paid in some other currency or medium. In answer to this objection, we may adduce the general disposition manifested on the part of all the best-regulated private banking houses, not only of this country, but of Europe, to use in their daily business, from which they grant loans and discount, circulating notes other than their own. This is especially the case in England, where the circulating notes are issued by the Bank of England.

The effect of this is to concentrate the reserve, giving greater security, and relieving all the other parties from the periodical discredits growing out of a drain of the precious metals. Previous to the war, the great bulk of the circulating medium used by the banks of New York City in the discounts and loans was not issued by them, but by other interior establishments,—the free use of certified checks effecting all the exchange of the city, their discounts and loans being made from capital and deposit.

The tendency of a circulation, if the issuing power is in the hands of the government, *will be to induce* capitalists and banking establishments to keep their *reserve* in *bonds*, knowing they can convert them into legal tenders at the moment of need. This is virtually discounting your notes in order to place them in some other channel. The specie reserve that is now kept on hand can all be used in loans and discounts. Now, when I speak of capitalists, I include the small balances over immediate consumption in the hands of all classes. All of their reserve will be invested in bonds, from the fact that they can wait until the day of need before conversion, and will not be forced to dance attendance on some director of a bank for a discount, which in time of need is not a certainty. By the inauguration of this cirtainty new life will be given to trade, enabling the whole country to sail close to the wind, and have but little, if any, reserve fund,—idle or useless to the country.

I hold that if a man desiring a discount, and in possession of a security to warrant a discount at bank, could go to a neighbor and borrow a bond on the same terms, the tendency of this would be to turn the attention of the country to the National Debt and renew the spirit of protection, and finally place bonds on a par with gold or any other four per cent. investment. The time may come when these investments may command a premium over any other government, from the fact that it is not only an investment, but one that will command a circulating medium and legal tender, both of which have their value in the market. There are times when secure investments are at a premium, or a low rate of interest, and times when a medium of exchange will command a premium. Now, if there be a conjunction of these favorable influences, it certainly will return a larger profit than either one can produce singly. Will not this consideration be taken into account by capitalists? It is their trade and business to note each item in the account of profit and loss, growing out of production and reproduction. When they cease to do this, investments will be at a discount, and accumulations a farce. The business of banking is distinct and independent of production when not speculative, but safely conducted. After all, whatever the medium may be by which the exchanges are effected, it is only the reproduction of capital or counters. The real capital of the country is the raw material, food, machinery, vessels, etc., and these absorb the entire business the community can carry on. After the recognition of a well-regulated currency is established, the facility of procuring discounts from a bank cannot increase or diminish their quantity. The same amount of values remain in the country and stimulate a corresponding trade, and can only affect the rate of interest, the result of which will be measured by the competition between lender and borrower.

It is only necessary that the government declare that legal tenders are equal to, or will be converted into, a gold-bearing bond of four per cent. interest, semi-annual, to give them a fixed value to that extent,—income being the measure of value. The fluctuations from this can only be to the extent of the current rate of interest, demanded by the course of trade and tendency to speculation. If this be the basis of their value, all will understand their worth, and so long as we give evidence of ability to pay four per cent., which can only be from an annual surplus, all investments will be based on this promise, and no great fluctuations can take place from ignorance of their value or how they are to be paid. This is all the government can do: no power can fix and keep unchangeable any legal tender or other commodity. They regulate themselves; if redundant on the market, the price or exchangeable value must sink. The converse of this holds equally good, and will bring appreciation, while the former gives depreciation. In order to have no fluctuations, from want of confidence, the government must make a promise she can keep, and then show a disposition to maintain it.

All I claim for this divorcement of the circulating medium from merchandise is, to free it from those periodical fluctuations incident to a foreign demand for the same medium. And as we are compelled to have in the exchanges of our internal commerce a medium, let us have the one most advantageous to the country. I claim, as equally economical, the vast saving to the country in the annual wear and tear in keeping up a medium so expensive as gold. This is no more than has been claimed by all modern political economists, from Adam Smith to Ricardo. They contended for a convertible medium, of paper, or something of less value than gold. And their views were engrafted upon the Bank of England, so far as to effect a separation of the *issue* from the *bullion* department. Under this system the greatest uniformity has been inaugurated, and full confidence in her notes for circulation.

The extreme wants of trade and pressure in two instances induced Parliament to remove, temporarily, the restrictions of the "Peel Act;" the necessity which called for this, each time, can be traced to causes other than those growing out of a paper circulating medium. Many causes, besides inflation or contraction, conspire to derange the affairs of commerce, especially where the circulating medium is convertible into gold on demand. A deficient grain crop in England, in the absence of a brisk demand for her manufactured goods, will cause a quick, sharp demand for the precious metals for export, gold being the only commodity left to offer foreigners, without a sacrifice, in exchange for food. And this must continue until the prices of other commodities, which they have for sale, fall to a point tempting speculation at home and abroad. During this interval the demand for gold must continue. Before this last resort comes, bankers and capitalists will call in from distant correspondents the last available dollar, and then only can relief be had.

Countries, like individuals, in times of diminished supplies may have to part with every available value to procure the means of existence, which must be had though the accumulations of years be exhausted in the purchase. Contingencies so unfortunate admit of no delay; and whatever exists of any other surplus must be parted with at the instant of want, however much the market may be depressed. Contingencies like this, with England so intimately connected with the great export article of this country, cotton, impose upon those looking to her for a market a large share of her misfortunes; consequently, prices may sink even below the cost of production, while her wants are being supplied with bread.

It is a well-established fact that when, from large crops and favorable seasons, the produce of a country is doubled, it will only sell for one-half of what it would provided the circulating medium were increased in the same ratio. It is in the inverse ratio to the supply, and can only circulate so much produce, and no more. Many will contend that, if this proposition hold good, half crops only should be made. They might as well insist on one-half a loaf being as good as a whole one. I admit that half a loaf is better than no bread, but it is not equal to a whole one. What I am contending for is that every one should be allowed the largest liberty in effecting exchanges, and not be confined to a particular measure of value; in a word, if I attend a fair at Newcastle, I may not be forced to take coals, but may have the liberty of taking my surplus to be exchanged for that of others. Many difficulties will suggest themselves to the minds of those who have never thought of a divorcement of money of account from an exportable article of merchandise like gold, and they will hastily condemn the scheme as wild and visionary. The defense and reasoning in behalf of the former will go far to quiet all fears and dissipate the anticipated evils which surround the dissolution.

For twenty-five years during the suspension of specie payments by the Bank of England, commerce and production grooved out their own channels, and felt but little if any inconvenience from the necessity which forced a recognition of a circulating medium whose value was only formed by the amount of commodities for which it could be exchanged, and not by the remote prospect of conversion into gold.

To have estimated their value on the contingency of the resumption of specie payment by the bank, the long delay being foreseen and fixed, would have given but a few cents value to her circulating notes. It was not the ultimate prospect of payment in gold which gave value to her notes, but the necessity of a circulating medium, and the consent of the producer to receive them in exchange for commodities and as legal tenders, thereby establishing a circuit in the exchange of commodities. This caused the barometer of trade to indicate the position of England's great surplus with certainty as unerring as though the circulating medium had been gold, without being subjected to the many charges of transfer from country to country. For three years after the suspension of the Bank of England, and so long as she was prudent in the issue of her notes, these notes were not only at par, but at times bore a premium of three per cent. over gold; and it was not until she, like others, entered into wild speculations that her notes fell below par. So soon as she reduced her amount of notes to the wants of a circulating medium, they again rose to par. By this reduction she apparently made less money, but in the aggregate, from a prudent circulation, realized more, without the same risk of impairing her capital. This demonstrates that paper money, if properly restricted, and recognized as legal tender, will answer all the purposes of gold for a circulating medium, without entailing on the country the wear and tear and loss by shipwreck in transportation from country to country.

It is now in the power of the government to effect this divorcement, without any change of policy except as regards the extension of it; and this extension will be subject only to the demands of trade. Nothing will be forced, but all for the interest of the people in lessening their taxes. If it is to the interest of the people to keep up the circulation of legal tenders to the full wants of the country, which it certainly is, as it lessens taxes, it is not to be presumed that the government will inaugurate a different plan, which instead of encouraging would defeat her efforts to produce a uniform currency, driving it in, and bringing on all the calamities of repudiation.

To estimate or look upon a national currency as suspicious or worthless, is not only national repudiation, but an evidence of individual disposition to discourage an honorable support of whatever the load of debt might be.

When the amount of issue is regulated by the supply and demand, and is uninfluenced by the prospect of individual gain, no overissue is likely to take place. With a free conversion of bonds into legal tenders, and *vice versa*, and a maintenance of ability on the part of the government to pay the interest with a prompt and honorable adjustment of the same, success will be guaranteed.

The foreign commerce of the country is now so large, requiring sums so immense at times for the liquidation of balances, that it becomes the duty of the government to divorce the internal commerce of the country from an article so variable in value as gold. If we continue it longer as the only legal tender and measure of value, and use it as a circulating medium, the periods of revulsion will soon be as fixed as the rising and setting of the sun,—up with large production, and down with years of scarcity. To say nothing of the legitimate demand incident to our foreign commerce, the growth of the spirit of speculation and gambling in the gold market, and the continual *bear and bull* influence brought to buoy up or depress the price, should be sufficient warning to the government that there can be no longer any safety in it as a measure of value or circulating medium. It will be ruinous to the best interest of the producing class to subject it to the daily fluctuations of an article which can be forced to vary from five to twenty-five per cent. in one day,—not in value nor from any legitimate demand, but wholly by the influence of the reckless spirit of a gambler. It certainly cannot be safe or secure to the commerce of a country to make it a measure of value when the speculative influences and gambling of a few capitalists can buy and sell four hundred millions in one day,—a sum almost equal to the entire exports of the country for one year, the legitimate demand of which would be only the difference between imports and exports, which ordinarily could not exceed five per cent. of this immense sum, or twenty million dollars.

The value of all articles being measured by the intensity of demand, the natural inference from a transaction so enormous would be that the whole world was short of gold, and was compelled to have it immediately, if the acquisition cost the last dollar of all other values. No one in his senses can be induced to think that this sum could or would be needed in the transfer of produce for consumption or reproduction. The idea is preposterous! The tenth part of this sum would bankrupt the Bank of England and the Bank of France, or cause their suspension. It now becomes the government, if it cannot remove the nuisance or incubus on production, to mitigate it, and not allow its baneful influences any longer to affect its legitimate collection of taxes and the payment of debts. A steady fixed purpose to liquidate to the last dollar, with the use of the greatest economy in all things, is its only financial duty. When, or where, or how much gold it shall sell in comparison with the gold clique, is not the question for consideration. The only influences which can honorably be brought to bear on all commodities should be such as are incident to its own wants, ways, and means. Then, under the rule of attending to its own business, the government will not be subjected to the fluctuations arising from the complications of others.

The attempt to apply a remedy to the wants of speculation is only inflicting a new wound to be healed. Let speculation adjust itself to its own wants.

FLUCTUATIONS—THEIR EFFECT.

The fewer fluctuations in the internal commerce of a country, the greater the security in the transactions and exchange of commodities based on present or future delivery.

When this is the case, the exports and imports will have to abide the fluctuations connected with their own transaction, each looking for their own safety and profit. This is precisely as it should be, and what I am now endeavoring to demonstrate.

The foreign trader deals with all countries on this basis of value or circulating medium, which is, after all, but bills of exchange, or in a transfer of credits. Hence the fluctuations that may attend them after the producer has parted with his property should not, by a reflex action on the circulating medium of the producer, cause him to share in the attendant losses.

If the original producer has his own independent circulating medium, he will not be involved in the fluctuations of other countries; nor will he have to share their losses, and can only be called upon to adjust and conform his surplus productions to the surplus of those with whom he wishes to effect an exchange. In a word, producers will measure values with values, neither of which will be affected by the medium used in effecting the exchange. Each party will profit or lose only by the over- or under-supply of their own circulating medium or standard of value.

If in this I have made myself clear, you can readily perceive the point or line of separation between values or commodities, and the circulating medium used in their transfer. The country having its independent medium of exchange will not be involved in the losses incident to a circulating medium common to all countries; nor can she be called on to participate in their speculations, even should it be their standard of value. We have seen that this can, without any assignable cause, be made to fluctuate twenty-five per cent. in one day, or involve one-quarter of a man's estate, should he be so unfortunate as to fall on that day in the footing-up of a maturing obligation.

Now, should any article of merchandise become superabundant by some wonderful process of production, or should a sudden calamity, as a great conflagration, cut short the supply in one day, then this great fluctuation would seem natural. In all candor, does it seem reasonable or just to retain a commodity like this as a standard of value, and call into the ring the honest producer with his hard-earned values, and force him to participate in its loss?—have his values measured by such a yard-stick, which, if not dishonestly clipped, has been immensely shortened?

For many years under what was called the mercantile system, which advocated and held that all wealth consisted of the precious metals, the idea was almost universal. The influence still exists over many minds; but the more enlightened portion of mankind have long since abandoned the fallacy, and estimate gold at its intrinsic value only, like any other commodity. So far as its purchasing power is concerned, it is owing to the influence exerted on the merchant or trader from the facility of a ready exchange for all other commodities that it is more sought after than other productions; and the fact that it is a legal tender, as well as a circulating medium, makes all men feel more at ease under maturing obligations, with the legal tender in sight, than they would with the possession of any other merchandise; hence the double desire to possess it, and also from the fear that it may be doubly important in time of need. This feeling is natural and instigated by the soul of honor and punctuality.

It is this indefinite influence which gives gold its principal value in exchange. There is no law beyond common consent to compel men to take it for their goods. If this be the case, it is precisely at this point its greatest value is fixed and given to it.

Strip it of this, and it settles down on its own merit, as a legal tender by law, to liquidate with, and not by common consent as a medium. In all other respects it is treated as a commodity, but with *reverence*. This arises from the fact that the majority of men and governments are debtors. Beyond this point all legal tender or measure of value is surplusage.

Man feels content under mere promises with this commodity in possession. When you sum up all, it is, as a legal tender, only applicable to the debtor, and cannot force the possessions or values of any man to change hands.

The purchase of bonds by the government at a premium is calculated to deceive, whilst it is urged as economy or cheapening the rate of interest, or that it will work a diminution of our taxes; so far from this, it is the purchasing of a new obligation, and the payment of the full interest for all the time the debt has to run to maturity. The case is not altered if the government should make a new loan at a less rate of interest. The burden of taxes will not be lessened from the fact that the full rate of the larger interest has been anticipated. The government is left in the position it would have occupied at the maturity of the bond and the acceptance then of the lower rate of interest. Precisely the same effect is produced by the collection and sale of gold, whatever may be the pressure. In neither of these is there either saving or economy to the country, but, instead, an absolute loss by the continual excitement and feverishness in all branches of trade, arising from the sale and purchase. All this may answer a purpose politically, and give men place and power for the moment. The least that can be said of its influence and effect is that it encourages and stimulates the most baneful species of gambling in every branch of trade—demoralizing to the best forms of society. None have power to condemn, as it is indorsed by the highest authority.

I admit that many difficulties surround this entire question which require time and a determined course to overcome. In order the more fully to understand and appreciate these difficulties we must look at our debt from a different stand-point, so that we may find means of extinction. Our debt is now a fixed fact, both principal and interest. It was created under circumstances the necessity of which no one will question. There was no time to higgle about rates of interest. The borrower was at the mercy of the lender. The money was to be had at all hazards, under all the disadvantageous circumstances surrounding the possible disintegration of the country. The rate of our principal debt could not reasonably have been reduced below six per cent. per annum. The promise of interest, however onerous, is now as much a part of the debt as the principal, and requires the same process of liquidation. This can be done only by a payment of both. The earlier it is done, the greater the economy. If we can, as we are entitled to do, borrow money at a less rate, say four per cent., this process will produce an absolute saving to the country of fifty per cent., interest being the measure of debt as well as of the value of incomes.

To effect this desirable end at an early day, and insure its easy accomplishment, we must show ability to pay not only the interest, but also the principal. There would be no difficulty in effecting a loan at four per cent. if the government, instead of selling gold, at once applied every dollar to taking up her bonds, which she now has the opportunity of doing, in accordance with the original contract; and open a loan at four per cent. gold, I feel confident that it would soon be taken up, especially if the promise to pay principal and interest in gold should be coupled with the engagement to convert them into legal tenders when demanded. Their fixed value, the entire closing up of the contingency of how and when they are to be paid, with the certainty of a conversion into a circulating medium whenever the demands of commerce require it, will give to the loan a double value to the full extent of the circulating medium.

I cannot but take this view of their worth when I cast my eye over this immense country, so prolific in all the commodities indispensable to man's wants,—unlike the productions ministering to luxury and ease, but such as will command the values of all nations and peoples.

When the capitalist looks upon this bond, yielding a fair and sure interest, and upon these great and increasing provisions for man's wants and necessities, and reflects that he can at any moment command them by simply converting the bond into legal tenders, he will tell you that it is the cheapest reserve fund he could keep by him, to command the fluctuations in rates of interest incident to commerce, springing from a deficiency in the food-crops of other countries. If a great famine should again stalk over the fair Emerald Isle, we would not then be compelled to pay freight, insurance, interest, and other heavy charges on gold to be sent here to purchase our bread. These items alone often amount to more than ten per cent., all of which would have to be paid or abated before we could send them our surplus in exchange for their surplus gold. This ten per cent. would be not only a loss to us in the price and value, but so much deducted from their bread, on account of the expensive medium which the merchant would be compelled to use in the purchase. Now, would it not be better that this sum should be divided between all the parties interested, realizing more to us for our produce, and giving to Ireland more bread? If the laws of legal tenders did not call on them for gold, which would derange the circulating medium, and perhaps bring on a panic, prostrating credit, a few of our bonds, if they had them, could be sent here and converted into legal tenders, and the proceeds sent to them in bread. Otherwise, the derangement of credit might so interfere with commercial affairs as to deprive the Irish people of the relief we were so willing to extend them. To effect this great saving not only to them but to us, however, a change in our legal tender or circulating medium is required. Another immense advantage to the country from this prompt payment of gold for bonds, not so readily seen, but surely to be felt, is the cheapening influence on *gold*.

The moment we abandon gold as a medium of value or a *circulating medium*, and throw it all on the market in the payment of bonds, its market rate will decline in all commercial centers, in the exact ratio of the extent of our currency and circulating medium as compared with those of all other countries which recognize the same standard of value. When we disburse one hundred millions of gold, the effect will be the same as if that sum had been vomited up from the mines without any of the expense attendant on the ordinary process of mining. And so long as we continue this process of collecting gold as revenue, and using it in payment of debt, so long will the credit and value of bonds appreciate in the market. In a word, it is not only the creation of a new value, but the use of it in the payment of debt,—giving evidence to the world that not merely can we command gold, but that we have the good faith to apply it at once to the liquidation of obligations in accordance with the stipulation in the bond. This system, honestly acted upon for a few years, will give to the country such credit that we may be able to negotiate a loan in gold at three per cent. Ability to pay, and the application of the means, will give to our national debt all the credit that can be claimed for the engagements of the most favored countries. Let us abandon this temporizing policy, this galvanizing of credit, this daily appreciation and depreciation of bonds and gold, and allow them to vibrate and fluctuate on their own merits, and to indicate their own worth by a steady stream flowing in the natural channel. The practice of throwing on the market large amounts of any commodity, and retiring securities, can have no other effect than to deter capital from seeking investment in either, whether permanently or temporarily, in a legitimate way of trade.

All operations now in gold or bonds are as hazardous as are the chances in a lottery or the gambling-room. Men will supply only their pressing wants, and will not be driven into the whirlpool of speculation, if they are seeking a sure and permanent investment.

Although they may neither desire nor be compelled to sell, they are unwilling to be forced daily to change the valuation of their investments. When prices are down temporarily, they must estimate their value at the market quotations. The timid man is inclined to part with his investment, and the bold one is not disposed to increase his; consequently a decline ensues, and for the moment the gambler comes in, on the principle of "make a spoon or spoil a horn."

I am well aware that no amount of argument or evidence can stay or influence a panic. Panics are controlled by no law, and must be left to exhaust themselves.

Let us return to the beginning,—the effort to economize in all directions,—which, after all, is the point of accumulation. Many things united conspire to this. The cheapening of a product by the introduction of new machinery not only redounds to the interest of the inventor or of the one using it, but is also a substantial blessing to all who are in any way connected with its products. To throw off this expensive medium — gold — and substitute a cheaper one, is to give to production a new capital, and also to cheapen the process of accumulation.

A country will become rich by diminishing its expenses on articles of luxury, and converting the savings into reproduction; it can never do so by dissipation and extravagance.

The use of labor-saving machinery to increase production is the ultimate end of all effort. It is an addition to enjoyment without a new expenditure,—an increase of wealth, and not of value. I prefer an increase of wealth from production, to accumulation from parsimony. The one adds to our enjoyments, the other deprives us of them.

The basis of all credit is confidence. This can spring only from ability, as I have already said. Capitalists are not likely to lend money to a country whose productions exceed but little, if at all, its consumption, whatever its past accumulations may have been. Without an annual accumulation and surplus above the supply necessary to a continuance of existence, no bolstering-up of public or private credit can or will last long. These devices and schemes of the financier will soon become threadbare, and leave the nation in a worse condition. In the history of a nation it sometimes becomes necessary to make use of an expedient for self-preservation. When the time for its use has passed away, it is equally incumbent to spare no effort of economy and stimulus to industry and enterprise, in order to resuscitate the income and bring it up to the annual expenditures. And if, after making an inventory of the ways and means, it is found that the accounts will not balance, still greater economy and energy must be used.

When individuals are staggering under a load of debt, they are willing to make an effort at throwing off their burden and arriving at better fortune, if the way be pointed out. Nations are not unlike them, and stand doubting, as if there were no energy in the land,—waiting for the word,—as did the United States when Kossuth appealed to it for men and money. Awhile all was doubt, until the orator, Henry Clay, spoke the word *non-intervention*. Not a man nor a dollar could then be had. Give to the people wise and just laws for the security of property and the protection of their rights, and production will soon build up the nation's capital and credit. After all, money, or the circulating medium of a country, is not so necessary to its welfare as is the abundance of the articles it will buy. Increase the food, clothing, etc. of the laborer, and reproduction will go on, even though there be no measure of value or medium of exchange.

The circulating medium being of no use except as a means for the exchange of productions, it becomes valueless when there are none to barter. Its office is then suspended, and along with other values it will be depreciated. This will continue as long as there is a dearth of commodities or capital. Whilst man has any wish unsupplied, there will be a demand for more commodities. So long as he has other values to exchange for them, the demand will be legitimate and effectual. Then, and not before, will he call to his aid the circulating medium or legal tender. It is auxiliary to man's wants, but otherwise incapable of supplying them. Production exchanges for production, but requires a medium for subdivision and distribution. Money in use is but the discoverer of the surplus of others. It is the pointer that finds the game; success or failure in securing the object depends upon the marksman. It ministers to the wants of speculation and production, in looking up articles necessary to their wants, and can serve no other end. It facilitates the exchange of all products; and if transportation has been cheapened and expedited, less money will be required, or a cheaper rate of interest will be submitted to.

On the other hand, if discounts or loans are needed, is it not far better that the government should effect them, by anticipating the maturity of a bond, receiving the proceeds in a uniform legal tender, than to be subjected to the uncertainty of obtaining them from a private bank, to the depreciation of their notes and the productions at the same time? The legal tender can never fall so low in value as any other promise or commodity. It is the desire to liquidate which causes an extraordinary demand for the legal tender as a circulating medium. Calamities flow from this want of a certain provision for the canceling of an obligation at maturity. But for this waiting for a settling-up of transactions, productions could be exchanged for productions, or be used in the liquidation of debt.

It is not customary in commerce to draw the true line between the legal tender of a country and the circulating medium. The difference is as great as that between pork and flour; one may be used in the absence of the other, and sustain life. The circulating medium is useful only in the exchange of commodities, the legal tender in the liquidation of debt or balances due on account. Withdraw the legal tenders, and the circulation of values will cease, except at a sacrifice in liquidation of obligation. So soon as they are canceled, a system of barter on the basis of supply and demand will be inaugurated; life will still be sustained, but it will be by the use of a very coarse bread. It is not the rude state of savage life, that knows nothing but barter, that I wish to see inaugurated; it is the adoption of a legal tender and medium of exchange indigenous to the country,—one that shall remain and be as constant as our capital stock and fixtures in trade, firm as the land we till, as fixed as the promises of the government to pay a four per cent. semi-annual annuity. The legal tender will then be consistent with the life of production, and will liquidate at all times precisely the amount of debt that it can command of commodities. When brought down to this point, all men's chances of profit will be alike; and when there is a depreciation in values below the cost of production or natural price, the legal tenders will depreciate to the same extent. The losses incident to all investments will then rest on the same foundation. One species of value will not have to pay a premium in order to create a sinking-fund to repair the losses incident to another. If capital seeks an investment in legal tenders, or the promise of them, in exchange for machinery or implements of production, and they should fail in giving a natural increase, from the want of which depreciation must follow, why should not a due share of these misfortunes attend the legal tenders? or why should they be called on, in addition to their own wants, to guarantee a never-changing legal tender, if it is of gold? Production never shares the profit, but is always required to make good the losses incident to its absence, when called for to liquidate. The chances are decidedly in favor of uniformity in the legal tenders of a country if used only as a circulating medium as demanded by the producers. This cannot be the case if gold, an article of merchandise, be used in the same capacity. The production and consumption of a country demand and create the one at the instant of want; the other is subject to all the delays and losses incident to its use by all other countries as a medium and legal tender. To command it at all times, even after submitting to the delays, you must offer an inducement, or sacrifice your values in exchange, if for no other reason than that of the sacrifice of their values by its withdrawal. It would never be parted with if what we offered in exchange was not of more value to the buyer than the gold. Now, if we should happen to be greatly in want of gold, and the countries with which we are offering exchanges of surplus should be equally in need, we would have to make an immense sacrifice to obtain it. Not so in case of a legal tender such as I have indicated, other than gold. The wants of all other countries for a circulating medium will not complicate our own misfortune. Our yard-stick will be at all times three feet long, and at hand to measure values or liquidate debt.

BILLS OF EXCHANGE—MODERN USE.

The purpose and aid to commerce of bills of exchange have been fully discussed by political economists, so far as concerns their application to the transfer of balances between distant points, thereby saving transportation and loss of time in effecting payments. I shall endeavor to explain the modern uses of them, and how far they exceed in magnitude all that has ever been claimed for them.

They are now the great motive power in effecting a circulation of all the values of distant and roundabout commerce. In fact, they play the same part in the distribution of the surplus of nations that the locomotive performs to its train of cars; their track is over mountains and deserts, they run all grades, make all curves, stop at all way-stations, and run through lightning expresses without change of cars; and, to make the comparison still more complete, they have their times of accident and disaster. A few illustrations from every-day life will, I hope, give to the uninitiated a clear view of the important part performed by bills of exchange in all the ramifications of production and consumption. Were they withdrawn from the commerce of the world, and all the transactions in commodities footed up in gold, one-fifth of all its shipping and transportation would be occupied in effecting the exchange and adjusting the differences.

Many without thought, and others even after reflecting upon the matter, are of the opinion that money is used in the purchase of our produce, that it is sent here by the buyer to pay for it on delivery. A greater mistake was never made. Not one dollar in one hundred thousand in gold is sent with the orders for our produce. All this will more fully appear as I advance in the elucidation of my subject.

When the spinner at Manchester wants or thinks he will need our cotton, he usually obtains a banker's credit, which he remits to his correspondent at New Orleans, with instructions to purchase for him, say five thousand bales of cotton if middling grade can be delivered in Liverpool at thirty cents per pound, gold, directing him at the same time to make his bills on the letter of credit at sixty days after sight and sell the same to any banker having the money. Before this order can be executed, the buyer must ascertain the rate of discount for his sixty-day bills, the rate of freight to Liverpool, local expenses, such as drayage, etc., his own commissions, classing, marking, and shipping, and then the price of cotton in the home market. All these items together will tell him whether he can fill the order. If not, he must await a decline either in the cotton or in some of the charges.

All the charges enumerated above come off the producer. And yet he has no further interest in the matter. It is nothing to him whether the cotton be paid for in gold or calico. He has received from his factor what he wants, something with which to pay taxes and debts, or to reinvest. I started this explanation with a letter of credit by means of which the cotton was purchased at sixty days. You will ask whence the banker got the money to pay for the sterling bill which was given on the letter of credit. He at once remits it to New York or London to his credit. The planter pays his debt to his country merchant, the country merchant pays his to the importer of the goods, and the importer or wholesale merchant in New Orleans goes to the banking-house and buys a bill of exchange on London or New York, which he sends to the manufacturer in payment of his debt or for the purchase of goods. Perhaps by the time this last bill on London is paid by the agent he has collected not only the sterling bill drawn against the cotton, but has purchased of the Manchester manufacturer a bill drawn on the New Orleans importer for payment of calicoes manufactured from this very five thousand bales of cotton. All of these transactions were effected without the intervention of gold.

Now, often this letter of credit and the authority to purchase produce are sent with what are called discretionary orders, and are frequently coupled with the injunction that the agent or buyer in New Orleans must take one-fourth or one-eighth interest in the profit or loss of the cotton when sold in Liverpool. This is done to secure caution in filling the order. Or it may be from a joint speculator in Liverpool, whose intention is to sell again to the spinner in Manchester.

I will give one more illustration of a *roundabout bill* of exchange.

A New Orleans speculator or importer of coffee obtains a letter of credit from a London banker, and sends it to Rio, on which bills at sixty days' sight are sold and the proceeds are invested in a cargo of coffee. When landed at New Orleans, the coffee is sold, and the proceeds are invested in a banker's bill and remitted to London to cover the sixty-day bill drawn at Rio. Or this New Orleans coffee operator may invest the money in cotton for account of the banker who gave the credit on Rio. In this way all parties are endeavoring to make a profit or commission from London *via* Rio and New Orleans.

Now, it is frequently the case, where parties have not the highest credit, that none of the above credits can be used except the cotton or coffee is consigned to the order of the banker or parties purchasing the bill of exchange. In the latter case they are called bills of lading exchange, and never sell at so high a rate, on account of the extra trouble of watching the transformations of the produce on which they are based. There is one observation I wish to make here, bearing particularly on the present course or system of exchanges. It is onerous to all growers of raw produce, and not so to the manufacturer, because all raw produce is taxed with the ruling rate of discount for sixty-day bills at the time of sale; in a word, all is sold on time, or, what is equivalent to it, as much less is paid for the produce before it can be sold as amounts to the discount on a sixty-day bill. The producer is forced not only to pay this discount, but he has to pay all charges of extra discount or premium for the discredit that may attend the sale of *time bills*, which is sometimes produced by a tendency to overtrade, or feverishness, that may influence capitalists.

It would seem as if there should be some compensation arising from this loss in some way; but such is not the case. If our importing merchants were allowed a corresponding credit on the manufactured goods, it would be some set-off; but instead of this they are required to deposit funds in advance, or a banker's credit, which amounts to the same, before the manufacturer will agree to execute their order. This, and the credit given them on the raw produce, frequently give ample time to work it up and fill the order.

From the above explanations in regard to bills of exchange and how they are used, and the immense part they play in the commercial affairs of the world, the natural inference is, that the speculator in produce and the dealer in bills of exchange are not one and the same individual. The buyers of produce on credits, or otherwise, are nothing more than drawers and sellers of bills based on the produce bought.

To this there are a few exceptions. The business has now grown to such magnitude that it is found most profitable to confine the dealing in bills to the banker and capitalist,—this being their business, they are better informed as to the degree of credit to be given to the parties drawing bills against produce. It is to them that all countries are indebted for the supply of gold and its general distribution over the world. They endeavor to keep all their money employed and paying interest, with the exception of that portion held in reserve.

If the current rate of interest in London be three per cent. per annum, and these large banking-houses find, from a want of money in New York or New Orleans, that they can purchase sixty-day sterling bills at a discount of three, four, or six per cent., they will not send the means to buy, thereby realizing in sixty or ninety days from nine to twelve months' interest. I have seen buyers of bills in New Orleans so short of money that eighty-two dollars would purchase one hundred and nine dollars in Liverpool; and I have seen checks on New York, drawn by dealers of the highest credit, sold in New Orleans at ninety-four dollars for one hundred dollars, and sixty-day bills at from ninety to ninety-two dollars. The parties drawing them stood so high in the New York markets that the notes were discounted at the rate of six per cent. per annum,—ample evidence that the low rate was not from want of confidence, but from the great scarcity of money,—and in a few weeks, so soon as gold could be had from Europe, the same bills commanded a premium.

In speaking of this sale of raw produce *on time*, and the purchase of manufactured articles *for cash*, I am reminded forcibly of a letter which an old-time merchant of New Orleans received from a new correspondent on the Mississippi River, requesting an invoice of sugar, coffee, and supplies, and stating that cotton would be forwarded by return of boat to pay him. He replied,—

"My dear Sir:—You begin at the wrong end of the line. Send forward the cotton, and the supplies will go by return boat."

Now, could the raw produce and the manufactured articles meet in *mid-ocean*, it would be only fair. Each party would have its own fluctuations to pay for. The only remedy—and that is but partial—is a cash business all around, or as near it as the transactions can be brought. In the language of Father Jones, when Simon Suggs gave in his experience, and spoke of wrestling with the serpent, *I've been all along thar.*

BALANCE OF TRADE.

In this connection I will notice a prevalent fallacy not only influencing the majority of individuals, but our national counsels. It is the much-talked-of influence of the balance of trade,—that it is favorable when it indicates more exports than imports, when nine times out of ten the reverse is what indicates prosperity and thrift. If A purchases in New Orleans one hundred thousand dollars' worth of cotton, and exports it to England, the entry on our custom-house books will be no more than this sum. When it arrives at Liverpool, many charges, such as freight, insurance, commission, etc., have been added, and, it is to be presumed, the usual profit; if this did not appear, A could not live and prosper. Suppose all these charges amount to ten per cent., which is hardly the average; now this credit represents in Liverpool one hundred and ten thousand dollars, and will be invested in a return cargo of calico, etc., which, at the invoice cost, will appear as an import at our custom-house for a like sum, and in the estimates of exports and imports will indicate a balance of ten thousand dollars against us, when, in fact, it is so much gain by our merchant, the true measure of which, the exchange or price of bills, will show no variation, and often, when the exchanges are favorable or unfavorable, the indication is only a desire on the part of one country to speculate in the other's goods. This will induce greater fluctuations and sharper competition than ever attend the liquidation of balances. The losses on the speculation, being often confined to parties unable to foot them, can cause no demand for exchange to cover the same, but must lie over to a more favorable season of speculation. The real capitalist in the trade asks but little credit; the speculator cannot get it. The prudent capitalist will not import long if there is not a demand for his goods, and this is generally the case when his customers have nothing to export; if they have nothing to sell, they cannot buy. There is no greater fallacy than the prevalent idea that there is an unlimited credit between the exporter and the importer. Should this to a certain extent be the case with a small portion of those engaged in the trade, it is to be presumed that if they know how to get into debt they will find a way to get out. And why the country that never pays one dollar of the losses should trouble herself continually as to the balance of trade when unfavorable,—when, in fact, it only indicates consumption beyond production, and will check itself and allow production to show an excess over consumption,—is difficult to comprehend. The true policy, and the only effective one, is to encourage industry and economy; the balance of trade will take care of itself. Individual speculators may have an unfavorable balance. To charge the collective commerce of a country with it is derogatory to the character of its mercantile intelligence. If a man exchanges one hundred dollars' worth of gold for one hundred and ten dollars' worth of flour, the balance of trade is certainly not against him, while he is in the enjoyment of the difference in the exchange.

APPLICATION.

I SHALL now proceed to sum up the foregoing arguments and reasons for a divorcement of gold from the circulating medium of our country, on the score of its fluctuations and unreliableness as a measure of value, from the fact that we are attempting to make it perform two offices, when the demand for it as a circulating medium by those who have it not, will or may be so intense as to incapacitate it for the moment as a correct measure of value for all other merchandise, or the liquidation of debt incurred with a view to its unchangeableness.

The greatest difficulty in its use as a medium or as legal tenders, is its absence when we want it, from the fact that other countries are using it in the same capacity at the same moment, and in order to attract it we must make sacrifices by forced sale of our substance in order to cover pressing wants.

Now, on the other hand, if we discard it as a legal tender in our own internal exchanges, and perpetuate the use of our present legal tenders, we will be at all times able to command them when we have arge productions or values to offer, without the depreciation of our property while waiting for the measure of value to be sent us from abroad. Our productions will still be the same, the medium or money of account can neither add to nor diminish quantity,—the producer will be left in the precise position he would have been in the liquidation of debts predicated on the future, that he would be if the promise had been to pay one bale of cotton or a barrel of mess-pork, and not be taxed with the rise and fall of any commodity other than the one he undertook to produce,—the proceeds of which were intended to cancel his obligation, to work out this relief; and to rid the producer of all risks not incident to his business by making his legal tenders such as will not be in demand by the Chinese, and beyond his reach when in demand, is certainly a great step to reproduction and incentive to renewed energies. He will not fail to produce when the depressing influence of exchanging one commodity for another—in order to make good a maturing obligation—has been removed.

This is the individual saving and view of the subject. The public gain is still greater, not only from their enhanced ability to pay taxes, but from the speedy lessening of the country's obligations, which of itself is adding to reproduction by the reduction of taxes.

Now, if there is a steady application of the available gold of the country, together with all that must be taken up on a four per cent. loan, to the payment of the onerous six per cent. debt, the credit of the new loan must appreciate, even should nothing more than the four per cent. loan be applied. The reduction of the debt will be fifty per cent. If one hundred and fifty millions be now required to pay the interest on a six per cent. loan, one hundred millions will pay it on a four per cent. debt. This certainly will be a great step in advance towards the liquidation of our large debt, and will place it on a par with gold, on the basis of the most favorable nations. Favorable as this view may be, it does not express one-half of the saving or absolute benefit derived by the government and people. Should the reduction steadily continue, by the payment of bonds, it will not be a great while—less than twenty years, indeed—before the immense and growing productions and commerce of the great centers of our country will demand and require a legal-tender circulating medium equal to the balance of our debt. There is a point where the two processes must meet. Absorption of the bonds by the requirements of a circulating medium, and actual payment on the other hand, are sure to come together. Suppose the point to be fifteen hundred millions of dollars. This country will then be out of debt and free from the assessment of taxes to pay interest; for how can the legal-tender circulation of the country be converted into interest-paying bonds when the absolute wants of production and commerce demand a circulating medium equal to fifteen hundred millions of dollars? No power is likely to deprive them of it. The demands of production and commerce are much more quickening than the slow accumulation of parsimony. Interest being the measure of debt, and the fifteen hundred millions of dollars paying no interest, it will be no longer necessary to levy taxes annually to meet it. So far as the government is concerned, the debt will be paid, as it will all be in the hands of its people. Every one of them using the circulating legal-tender medium will carry his own share of interest. The circulating medium will then be truly a great mutual benefit association for the protection of all. The fortunate holders will bear the losses of those who are so unfortunate as to have nothing to offer in exchange. The accumulated premiums are the lessening of taxes, all of which will be annually divided out in legal tenders, and not in scrip of indebtedness or bonds.

The conclusion I make from the foregoing is, the practicability of the payment and liquidation of the entire debt—twenty-five hundred millions of dollars—before its maturity, with the payment of only six per cent. interest per annum, or one hundred and fifty millions of dollars. The reduction this will make on the one hand, and the absorption into legal tenders on the other, will soon create a credit equal to a four per cent. annuity or loan, and all combined will bring the extinguishment in less than twenty-five years, and give to the country a uniform currency and *legal tenders*. The plans to secure this desirable end can easily be given.

CONSOLATION.

Amidst all the disasters and sacrifices which the late war involved, almost the entire amount of the immense capital required to carry it on was produced by the country. The amount loaned or furnished by other countries would not have defrayed the expenses of one campaign. This large sum loaned to the government by its people was produced by them under all the disadvantageous circumstances of the withdrawal from the legitimate labor of production of over one million of men. If we could sustain this large consumption during the four years of the conflict, and come out of it with ample means to prosecute other and more profitable, but quite as gigantic enterprises, coupled with increased production, it certainly should console us under the burden of debt, especially when it represents so small a portion of the values consumed, the balance having been contributed each year in the shape of taxes. Now, if energy and enterprise can create and spare, without impairing production, five thousand millions in four years, how long a time will it require the same people, under increased facilities, to cancel one-half the sum by the savings from their surplus? It certainly will be but a very small percentage if gathered from twenty years. When we think of these immense sums, and of the shortness of the time which was allowed for their creation, we cannot be otherwise than thankful to the Giver of all good for so prolific a country. It is a fortunate producing country that can add to its capital stock ten per cent. per annum over consumption, but how much more fortunate is the land that can not only lay up this percentage, but can loan and contribute to its government one thousand millions annually, and a million of soldiers to fight her battles!

LEGAL TENDER.

To give paper money currency at par with gold, is to limit the supply to the wants of a circulating medium. To effect this, the power to issue only in exchange for bonds will not inflate the market. It is not reasonable to suppose that the holder of bonds will go out of them into any money or other commodity the tendency of which is toward depreciation. If, on the other hand, he feels impressed that there is a redundancy of money, so far from converting bonds into legal tenders, he will convert his legal tenders into bonds. In this way the equilibrium will be preserved without the continual influences surrounding the issue of paper money generally. The government, issuing legal tenders only for the benefit of its people, will have no inducement to increase the issue, knowing that all beyond the amount necessary to form a circulating medium will return to be invested in bonds. This will be the national barometer, indicating the rise and fall in the circulating medium of the country with as much certainty as the rise and fall in exchange show the state of the debits and credits of one country with another.

The loss to the individual holder of legal tenders when the market is overstocked with them will be to the extent to which they would have accumulated while in his possession with no commodity for which to exchange them indicating a future profit.

It is to be presumed that the holders of legal tenders will fully understand the difference between them and government notes bearing interest, and that, in looking round for an investment when the circulating medium is no longer profitable, they will naturally turn to bonds. This facility of earning an interest on the small individual surplus of the country will induce habits of economy in all classes, not only in the consuming but in the producing.

Nothing tends so greatly to the growth and internal prosperity of a country as the formation of such habits; the very savings will induce further production, in order to, as it were, compound them.

It is unjust and illiberal toward the producing portion of the country to tax it with the whims of the miser or the wild schemes of the speculator, in order to make the circulating medium of a country not only secure but unchangeable in itself when compared with all other productions of value.

If the miser wishes to hoard his savings and lock them up from the use of commerce or reproduction, it is not to the great productive interest of the country to pay him a bounty in the shape of extra security of unchangeableness, in order to retard the general progress of society in the accumulation of something further for consumption.

It is not the miser who builds up a country. He hoards his earnings, and whilst so withdrawn from the world they are as dead and unproductive as if cast into the sea. The prosperity of a country consists in its production and consumption, and not in a destruction of values by hoarding them up after the manner of Captain Kidd.

The accumulation of values not used in liquidation and not liable to decay is well enough in its way, but is admissible only when the productive energies of a country have been pushed to their utmost capacity. Opulence, dissipation, and decay will follow,—in a word, a country then begins to *live on its seed-corn.*

To stimulate the merchant and the man of commerce by fair laws and wise and just regulations, is the duty of every country which has increasing desires and wants to be supplied; but to insist that production should guarantee that any one commodity should remain invariable, and be at all times exchangeable for a like quantity of other products of value, is unreasonable. It would be more honorable to guarantee to the producer a uniform price or exchange for his surplus. It is not to be supposed that he is thoroughly conversant with values and the many changes continually affecting commodities. He is not on the watch-tower, and must rely on the honesty not less than on the wisdom of the trader for his knowledge of the condition of markets,— where there is a glut, and where a scarcity can be found for his surplus. The circulating medium of a country, if legal tenders, measures the value of all commodities; from this comes its use as money, and as a security it is a tacit mortgage not only on production but on all the capital-stock, lands, and tenements of its people. It is unlike the bonds of the nation, which are payable at a distant period, and bear only on surplus production. When this fails, not only does the interest cease, but the bond has no security and becomes worthless; for how can unproductive property, or such as produces only maintenance of its occupants, be considered security? All property is measured in value by the annual income.

WHO PAYS THE EXPENSE AND CHARGES OF A MEDIUM.

It is well known that gold, like all other commodities, is continually seeking the country that is willing to pay the highest price for it. No country in want of it can command it without valuable commodities, and not even then without offering to a certain extent to sacrifice them; when it has been obtained, at whatever cost, the gold is only, after all, a legal tender in the payment of debt, and will not afterwards command any of the conveniences and necessaries of life, any more than it would have done had this sacrifice not been made to procure it as a legal tender, which might serve as a medium of exchange, to effect the sale and transfer of domestic products, many devices could have been resorted to before submitting to this loss, incident to the providing of a legal tender. Any kind of counters would have been used, such as checks, bank-notes, or open credits, and the transfer of valuables. Every market-town would be a clearing-house for the surrounding country, and cause the debits and credits of each producer to be liquidated. After all that can be said or done, the history of production and consumption is but book-keeping by double entry: whenever a credit is given a debit must be made; whatever comes in is debtor to that which goes out; when you compare the debit side with the credit, and find them equal, you feel confident the postings have been made correctly. Now, if you will examine the balance-sheet carefully as you close up the accounts by profit and loss, you will find the heaviest charge is for legal tender, and that the export articles of the country are charged with the entire amount. Although the largest item in the great ledger, you are convinced it is correct, from the fact that exports pay for imports, with all the charges incident to the trade.

Now, if the exports of a country have to pay all the charges and expenses of a legal-tender medium, is it not all-important to this interest to have them cheapened in every possible way with a due regard to safety? This is not all. If exports lose five per cent., or five dollars on each one hundred dollars, and the exports of the country should sum up five hundred million dollars, twenty-five millions less of imports can be commanded, or, in other words, the producer of export articles will be deprived of consuming domestic goods to the amount of twenty-five millions, or of the turning of it into reproduction; in whichever way you view it, it is a loss to the country, besides lessening the demand for home-made commodities.

I have met with no work on political economy urging this fact, connected with the exports of a country. Instead of this, you will find the producers of exportable articles claiming all the credit for enabling their country to resume specie payment, and even that they will force this legal tender to be used, and set up for themselves until others do the same. All I can say is, they have not examined the account, and picked out the important item of twenty millions of dollars, or one-twentieth of their gross income. The country that can stand this charge and prosper must be peculiarly favored, but is blind to its own interest in not forcing all productions to pay *pro rata* for a legal tender. If the exports of a country support the charges incident to a legal tender, the producer should use all honorable means to lessen those charges. To do this it is unnecessary to make war on any interests, since all productions are alike interested, the exports directly and the imports indirectly.

In conclusion, I can only give the advice of Joe Nash, the bar-keeper on the steamer Natchez, who, when he found a "big-fisted fellow" stealing apples from his barrel on the guard of the boat, at once pitched into him, but stated afterwards that he could have whipped him much more easily if both arms had been in the barrel. When you want satisfaction, be certain both arms are in the barrel.

If you cannot import without having something to export, how can the legal tender be bought or brought into the country? Confine the circuit of the medium and legal tender to our own country, then all parties desiring it will have to pay in the proportion which their products bear to the volume of the medium and the supply of all other commodities.

In order to make this position clear to all, let us take the case of a producer of cotton,—a constant commodity of export. We will suppose his profits to be a fair average of production over consumption, say ten per cent., and the production one hundred thousand dollars. In order to realize from this the market rate in the legal tender or circulating medium, the exporter must be able to negotiate his bill of exchange through a banker against the anticipated proceeds of this cotton in the foreign market. To do this (as I have previously shown) he must submit to an average discount of five per cent., or five thousand dollars. Who are benefited by this loss to the producer? It is not the *spinner;* for he has to pay the same price, or else the exporter would not have been able to pay the five per cent. discount. The benefit is shared by the entire country, from the banker down to the humblest recipient of the legal tender or medium of exchange. It matters nothing to the producer or to the country whether the proceeds come back in gold or in calico, there is no difference if the demand require it,—one is a legal tender, the other a liquidator, either closes up debt and liabilities. Not one dollar may have been needed for a legal tender—gold. Still, as the business of the country was conducted on that basis, for fear it might be called for, the charge was made.

If you register your name and take a room at a hotel, you have to pay; whether you eat and sleep there or not, it is the business of the hotel-keeper to have meals and a bed in readiness for you. So the dealer and banker will tell you he must be ready to pay the legal tender or a simple transfer of credits; however you turn the export, the producer has lost five thousand dollars, and all the other producing interests of the country for domestic consumption have been furnished with a legal-tender horse to ride all the year free of charge. There is no remedy, on a gold basis, to save the producer of export commodities this heavy loss; he is precisely in the condition of the speculating bank issuing notes as a medium convertible into coin on demand,—he must at any sacrifice be ready to pay, whether called on or not. If the imports balance the exports, no gold will be required. Still, the five thousand dollars must be paid, as a premium or tax for the privilege of acting as a financial agent of the country. No benefit can arise even should the producer's ten per cent. profit come back in gold; if wise, he will lay it out in pork or flour, to extend and aid reproduction. The proceeding, so far as the large discounts have been submitted to in order to procure a gold medium, is applicable to the time previous to the inauguration of the legal-tender act of 1862, or when gold was the measure of value and legal tender, and, in my humble opinion, is conclusive against gold; but, in order to make the proof clear, and at the same time do justice to our present medium and to the wisdom of the legal-tender act, I have only to refer to the New Orleans and New York quotations for rates of exchange drawn against exports. At the former point bills are made against cotton exports, and at the latter they are consumed by imports. Can you point to a single week of discount for sixty-day bills exceeding three per cent.? In no eight years in the history of this country can there be found so few fluctuations from the gold measure. This fact is due alone to gold being no longer a legal-tender medium. I have not the data at my command, but will venture the assertion that there has not in any single instance been a variation exceeding two per cent., and even that has been but for a very short period; this, too, in the midst of a dearth of gold, growing out of the extreme wants of the country in the absence of its leading export article, cotton. The quotations in New York a few days ago (March, 1870) fell to eight per cent. for good bankers' bills in London. This was stated to be in consequence of heavy shipments of cotton from the South to Europe, and a pressure of bills drawn against this cotton in the New York market, in consequence of which the rates fell from eight and one-half and eight and three-quarters, being about the season average. Only a limited amount of the sterling bills sold in the New Orleans market against cotton are remitted to London and drawn against direct. The great bulk is forwarded to New York for sale, and sight checks are drawn against proceeds from New Orleans. New York, being the large importing point, attracts all the bills against exports for consumption by importers. In the New Orleans quotations for sight checks on New York, the fluctuations rarely ever exceed one per cent., the ruling rates being near par, or an amount barely sufficient to cover the express charges on legal tender, and the usual bankers' commission. Previous to the war, when gold was the medium and legal tender, bank-checks on New York were frequently sold in New Orleans at from six to eight per cent. discount,—at times could not be sold at all. Can better evidence be offered in favor of a continuance of our present legal tender, and a permanent divorcement from gold as an internal measure and medium of exchange? If referred to at all, let it be as a remote measure, in order that the balance between our imports and exports may be adjusted in conformity with the legal tender of the countries with which we are in correspondence. Allow all parties who may so desire, or who are required to do so by the wants of their particular trade, to issue gold, pork, or flour notes, but at the same time allow the people of the interior to use their own legal tender in the exchange of their productions. If in possession of value, they will at all times be able to find it, without being forced to pay a tax to some one to import it from China. Let the measure be at all times alongside of their commodities. Quick sales, without unnecessary reductions consequent upon the use of a false and variable medium, will enable the producer to return all the sooner to his work and commence reproduction again.

During the prevalence of the mercantile system, among many other errors in production, consumption, and distribution of wealth, laws and restrictions of all kinds were enacted to prohibit the exportation of the precious metals. The statute-books of England, France, and nearly all other commercial nations are filled with prohibitory laws; so that one not better informed might imagine that gold and silver constituted the meat and bread of the people, and that without an abundance of these commodities all would soon be brought to starvation. This policy has long since become extinct with all commercial nations. Still, I regret to say, a large majority of the great mass forming those nationalities cling to the idea that all wealth consists of gold, and that no great prosperity can be expected by a people that has not the bulk of its valuables invested in this metal. Even enlightened law-makers in our legislative halls are now urging the government to devise some plan to prevent the gold products of California from being sent off. From the enthusiasm with which this measure is urged, one might be led to believe we were giving gold away, or that we were at least receiving nothing of value in exchange. In my opinion the producer has the best right to judge of his own wants and interests; and if he is prospering in the mining, the machinery and implements to increase production will find a place in his orders. Production stimulates and provides for consumption. Good example and moral teachings will direct it in the best channels for the government of society. The prohibitory law to prevent the one will extinguish the other. If you give to society the command of luxuries and amusements, teach them that it is a sin to abuse the gift. The moment you attempt arbitrarily to restrain, you awaken the turbulent and unruly passions of man's nature.

INSTINCT.

It is wonderful how faithfully Nature prompts us to the truth, and how persistent she is in urging us on to the correction of error; from this I am led to believe that man's nature is not wholly evil, but that, if led astray for a time by selfishness and temptations, it will finally right itself, although, it may be, not until the mischief is glaring and great.

I have been led to this train of thought and reflection by looking back no farther than the seventeenth century. Up to its close the edicts of the mercantile system, with all its errors, shaped the legislation of all Europe, and influenced the commercial relations of the most astute minds. One of the prevailing fallacies (to sustain which the statute-books are filled with laws) was that all wealth consisted of gold; and to retain it or cause its import into a country was the chief end of the legislation and wisdom of man. In the year 1663, however, England gave this great error the death-blow by rendering the export and import of gold as free as those of all other goods, thus overthrowing the dogma and asserting that wealth consists in abundance.

If you will take into account the outside influences controlling all this legislation, you will see the *spark of truth*, the *beacon-light* still directing our course. Gold had been by law and convention made the circulating medium, legal tender, and measure of value for all property and productions; to allow its export was to place all interests at the mercy of its return,—or to establish between the measure and the production an unnatural proportion, subjecting all values, whether in exchange or in the payment of debt, to ruinous sacrifices. It was this grain of truth that occasioned the struggle for prohibitory laws to restrain the export, under the belief that no more would be brought into the country than was necessary to circulate its products and liquidate debt. To have retained in the country an adequate sum would have mitigated and lessened all the evils of a contrary course. The true principle was not seen,—error had to correct error. I am forced to side with *instinct*, and favor the legislation that will retain in the country a uniform sum of the legal-tender medium, and not unnecessarily permit its exportation in the face of a home promise that it should be present on demand, or should be at all times equal to the commodities offered in exchange, or debts based on the same to be canceled.

We have only to look to our own legislation, no farther back than 1862, the date of our present legal-tender act, all the credit of which has been ascribed to necessity and the perils then surrounding our country. If the truth could have been perceived,—what nature was endeavoring to work out and demonstrate in regard to a medium of exchange,—the prohibitory law of 1864 against gold would never have been enacted. Now that we have laid hold of the truth, let us adhere to it.

If gold is to be the medium and measure of value, let us imitate the wisdom and magnanimity of the legislator from Maury county, Tennessee, who, when importuned by the member from the adjoining county, Hickman, to pass a law prohibiting the people of Maury from *grazing* their *cattle* in his county, moved an appropriation of funds sufficient to *fence* in the *county* of Hickman. Nothing more was ever heard of this subject or of the grievances of the people of Hickman. If we are to go back to gold, then let us fence it in, and regulate the amount of stock to the pasturage.

GOLD—LEGAL TENDER AND CIRCULATING MEDIUM.

There are two agencies constantly at work whose tendency it is to destroy the relation between the value of gold and that of all other commodities, thus impairing its efficiency as a measure of value or legal tender. One is the natural increase from mining; the other, the expansion of production. The former cannot be stimulated to any great extent by the influence of the demand, even should it be an extraordinary one. New mines cannot be found at will. New fields can be opened and cultivated in grain at the moment of the effective demand for consumption. There is an annual indicator, which prompts men to increase or decrease production. Not so with gold, which can be consumed only as a medium of exchange. The articles exchanged cannot be dispensed with, but the medium can. The ablest statisticians and political economists have differed widely as to the supply of gold now in the world; even as to the amount in France there is a difference of twenty-five per cent. in estimates. How, then, can capital know when to increase production, the indication of supply being so vague? Speculation cannot prompt capital to the increased production of gold. The only sure guide is the finding of large nuggets in new fields. Then there is a rust not only of capital, but of poverty. We read of a bird that swallows its food without mastication, and digests the same without nutrition. The benefit is not apparent, as there is no increase in bulk. The effect of gold is precisely the same. With all the wear or loss and the ornamental uses to which it is put, the consumption is thought to be not over five per cent. All other commodities, especially food, are consumed within the year. How, then, can gold, an unknown quantity, be a constant measure of a decreasing commodity?

If the amount of gold in any country could be confined to the wants of a circulating medium, without increase or diminution, except so far as the exchanges required it for increased production, it would be a reliable legal tender and measure of value. But to allow it, as is now the case, to be all attracted to one country whilst the productions of the country are being harvested and exchanged, is to enhance its value in the country deprived of it,— which has maturing obligations incident to former prosperity. The effect would not be so disastrous if the gold were only wanted as a medium to effect exchanges; other substitutes and devices can be used to facilitate circulation, but as a liquidation the pound of flesh will be insisted on. Cannot the labor of man, and the industry and enterprise of a great country like this, be guaranteed from the ever-recurring loss?

The vicissitudes of life bring in their train enough of want and misery, without compelling men to insure capital against any portion of the losses incident to reproduction. When men put their merchandise on a frail bark at sea, if unable to stand a loss, they insure against the perils incident to the voyage. Why should not the capitalist, when he loans to labor the reproduction of one barrel of pork, be forced to pay a premium to some one willing to cover his risk, or stipulate with the borrower that if, on his return of the tender or representative loaned him, it will not command one barrel of pork, he will look to him for the difference,—while, if it commands more, he will share the excess with him? This is what I call "an eye for an eye, and a tooth for a tooth."

I do not wish to be understood as being unwilling to give to capital every guarantee, both of law and equity, of a full return of all the value loaned, together with such profit as will fully cover all risk and insure a fair increase: I simply desire to protect labor against the disastrous effects of the legal tender, gold, being out of the country at the maturity of the obligation; and this can be done in no better way than by substituting something that is not more likely to leave the country, than a man would be to part with his bread and meat to-day when he is sure to need them to-morrow.

In my judgment, it would be far more conducive to production to have no law which should compel the payment of any legal tender, than it would be to force a man to procure gold at the sacrifice, it may be, of all his earthly possessions. It certainly would be more just to the laborer to allow him to return to the capitalist such values as he borrowed. The gold lent was only an order, or the purchasing power of so much food and raiment, on the merchant. And if this is returned with the ordinary profit or interest for its use, it seems but just and fair, and frees the laborers of the country from subjection, in the language of the stock exchange, to a corner that may be made in gold by capitalists. If gold could be relied on in its production to indicate the value of a day's work as a legal tender or medium of exchange, more reliance could be placed on its unchangeableness as compared with other commodities. This is far from being the case if gold is not where it is needed: values not alongside of each other cannot measure values accurately, since they are different in different countries. As a medium of exchange, how can it be prudent or just to measure value by it or call it a legal tender? So far from its being a constant indicator of the value of labor, it is so generally worshiped that the most insane projects are set on foot to obtain it. A short time ago, there was a bill before Congress asking the loan of a large sum to aid a great mining company, stating that the mine had heretofore yielded sixteen millions of dollars, but that now, with forty-two engines constantly pumping water, and other expenses, the annual cost of producing this sum amounted to seventeen millions of dollars. I should call this throwing one million dollars into the sea, to say nothing of the increased production that would result from the employment of such a sum in any other pursuit. If seventeen millions of dollars were expended to secure sixteen millions of dollars' worth of provisions to obtain subsistence for human beings, the propriety of the outlay would be sufficiently evident; but to prosecute the mining of gold at the cost of so large a sum,—expended not in food for the poor, but in food for an *engine*,—when so many human beings are willing to toil for subsistence, seems to me an indication either of lunacy or of the grossest selfishness: it is not the increase of capital, but accumulation in the hands of the few at the expense of the many. An enlightened philanthropy would prompt the employment of capital where it would minister to the largest number of human beings dependent on it for a supply of the comforts of existence, rather than use it in such wasteful enterprises and in undertaking to set up such golden gods. Such a system of investment would, in sixteen years, extinguish the entire capital, that might have been used in reproduction and in the continuance of our species. Far better would it be to forego the toil and losses of the mine and roam the forest in search of the precarious subsistence from its game.

It is not from its increase that gold derives its interest; it is the increase of commodities to be exchanged by it that regulates the charge of interest. If with one thousand dollars I can command the subsistence for the reproduction of eleven hundred dollars, I certainly can afford to pay more for its use than if ten hundred and fifty dollars were the expectancy of yield. The borrower or middle man must have some margin for a profit; if not, he had better fall back on his own labor for the means of a continuance of existence. It matters not what direction be given to capital, the employment must yield more than the interest promised, or it will cease to be used, and will become valueless. Hence the intimate connection between capital and labor—the decrease of the former will impoverish the latter, and the prosperity of the latter will give security and increase to the former.

If the government, which has the power to regulate the currency and money of the country, would look as closely to the regulation of the supply as the wants of trade require, the value and its measure would regulate themselves, and the debtor class—almost the only one affected by legal tenders—would be saved numberless losses and sacrifices in retiring their maturing obligations.

The medium of exchange, or circulating medium, adjusts itself to the values presented in exchange. No one is compelled to part with his production for it, if he does not consider it an equivalent. Not so, however, if obligations have to be met: it matters not how great the sacrifice, the legal tender must be procured. Every one is aware of the fact in the exchange of commodities, that if both parties are not in want in the same degree, concessions must be made by one in order to induce the other to change his investment.

Why the government, that undertakes to regulate the medium and legal tender of a country, and enacts the laws necessary to enforce the performance of contracts, however inconvenient it may be to the debtor, should not, at the same time, place a legal tender within the debtor's reach, one that he can command when he has values to exchange, I am at a loss to perceive. The commerce of a country would go on the same, and quite as many enterprises of production would be entered into, since it is not the legal tender loaned or borrowed on time that sustains labor, but the loan is really the production that it will exchange for. It will probably be said, in answer to this, that foreign countries will not take our legal tenders for their engines, steam-plows, etc.; but if we have commercial values, such as cotton, flour, pork, etc., we shall be able to command all we need, or are entitled to, just as certainly as if we had the gold. Furthermore, how can we obtain the gold if we have no valuable production to offer in exchange? When produce is purchased with gold, the one is as much a purchasing power as the other: the only difference between the two arises from the law having given to the one the power of a legal tender in the discharge of debts.

If this plan of a local legal tender be adopted by the government, the time will soon come when other countries will have something else than gold as a medium acceptable to us in exchange for our breadstuffs, cotton, etc., from the fact that we will give preference over gold to commodities suitable for reproduction. When we give a bill of exchange against our values, it commands the legal tenders of the country upon which it is drawn. What more can we ask? Their legal tender will command their production, the relative value of which was fixed and entered in the cost of the production given for the bill of exchange.

The adoption of two legal tenders, in a great country like ours, will not be a difficult matter,—

the one for the circulation of commodities and payment of debt in regard to all our internal transactions, the other to meet foreign wants. If the merchant who deals with a foreign country, as well as with our own people, should have to procure a legal tender acceptable to that country, it is his business to inquire into the nature of the particular commodity promised. If the legal tender of our country will not cancel his obligation, he must exchange it for one that will. If there is no such value in the country, all that can be said for him is that he has not exercised the forethought which makes sure of a buyer's ability to pay, before delivering goods to him.

Prudent merchants will not give credit if production is not going on and the debtor is not likely to have the means of payment. To encourage debt in a non-producing people is a crime, and the sooner the traders are brought to bankruptcy the better for the country. The greatest losses incidental to trade grow out of temporary speculation in one or two commodities in the expectation of a rise: if the expectation prove fallacious, losses and bankruptcy will follow. If the reverse be the case, the fortunate bull will be the gainer of the bear's portion. After the combat is over, there will be the same amount of productions in the land as before, and they will settle down to their natural price when exchanged the one for the other. Speculation, or the inflation of the medium of exchange, does not diminish or increase the relative value of commodities generally: seldom are more than one or two excited at the same time. When the epidemic has run its course, the relative value of pork and flour, or of cotton and gold, will be found the same. There may be many wrecks by the wayside, but the same capital, the same sustaining power of production, will be in existence, and will be applied to reproduction, when the storm is over. The inflation of values may have brought sore distress on many, but one year's supply will be left to stimulate increased production.

In calmer times, when speculation has not usurped the place of production, the values of all commodities are measured in exchange with each other by the amount of labor required to bring them into existence. Beyond this all is speculation, bringing profit to the fortunate holder, or entailing countless loss on the many who are the dupes of men who live by their wits rather than by their labor. Capital does not often open out these speculative channels, or look to them for a return for its use; but it is frequently drawn into the whirlpool, and at times its owner is involved with it. The earnings of the poor, to a large extent, will be absorbed. I can suggest no remedy for this state of things but a cash business. Then the honest earnings of one man would not be sacrificed to pay the losses of another.

There is, in times of panic, a sort of instinctive impulse in the mind of man to hoard up gold. This disposition is increased precisely in the ratio of the intensity of the panic. All this happens at a time when debtors are least able to bear the burden of the enhanced value of the legal tender To withdraw gold from circulation, even temporarily, is to increase its exchangeable value. Whatever this may be, the entire burden is thrown on the debtor portion of society, and seldom results in any substantial gain to the creditor or lender of capital generally. It is the speculator that takes advantage of the occasion to buy in the bargains, either to hold them or to profit by the necessities of the laborer. Production is retarded by the stagnation of articles of consumption, and this state of things must continue until an equilibrium is established between the legal tender and production. The effect is to make the laborer poorer and the capitalist richer by the periodical withdrawal of the medium, or legal tender, from the market, and the absorption that must follow this depression of commodities and the enhancement of the medium while liquidation is being effected.

All this is continually passing in review, and yet we continue, with a blind idolatry, the worship of gold, when every one knows that it is absorbing productive capital in its mining, being itself unproductive. The measure of its value is the labor consumed in its production : why not direct this labor to the accumulation of wealth,—"the necessaries, conveniences, and enjoyments of human life," as so aptly defined by Adam Smith?

One circumstance in connection with gold should always be kept in mind. When it is adopted by a country as a legal tender or a circulating medium, it is not sent to that country, by the banker or trader in it, until exportable values have fallen to a price sufficiently low to attract it. The first indication of this is the discount on bills of exchange drawn on the great points of export; it is not alone this discount on the bills which tempts the dealer in gold to supply the demand for the sake of profit, but further concessions must be made, to allow the trader or exporter a reasonable chance for profit. The margin in these times must be wider than in the ordinary course of trade, to cover the enhanced risk incident to the excitability of the market. When cotton was selling at eight or nine cents per pound, the buyer or seller would haggle over one-eighth or one-thirty-second of a cent in price; now that it is selling at twenty-five cents, we seldom see a quotation of an eighth, one quarter, or one-half: one cent is looked upon as but a slight concession. And so it is with all commodities: as prices become excited and enhanced, the *selvedge* must be *widened*.

The estimated loss to England per annum in the maintenance of a metallic circulating medium amounts to no less than $20,000,000, and that to France amounts to $30,000,000, estimating the rate of interest at five per cent. and the wear and tear at one per cent. These are large sums with which to tax the commerce of a country, especially when there is added to them the further sum that could be realized from a prudent investment in reproduction. It is impossible to estimate what the tax would have been had it not been for the continuous exertions of commerce to supply a cheaper circulating medium by calling to its aid banks of deposit, banks of circulation, checks and bills of exchange (the latter being now used almost exclusively as the purchasing power between countries). After all these devices and improvements to facilitate the exchange of commodities, we find the two most enlightened commercial nations laboring under this heavy subsidy,—a sum which would provide for the comfortable maintenance of their entire poor. In the face of this great outlay, who will advocate a continuance of this wasteful idol-worship, when a substitute answering all the purposes and in a more expeditious manner can be found without bringing in its train this heavy loss to productions? All banking and commercial history teaches us the nature of the struggle that has been going on in all countries to effect economy in the circulating mediums, and the many devices employed, in the then existing state of production and enterprise, to simplify and adapt them to the necessities and wants of trade. Without many of the improvements engrafted on the mediums of the past, production and consumption could never have reached their present elevated position, the necessaries now enjoyed by the poor would still be luxuries far beyond their reach, the rude cabin would still occupy the place of the stately mansion, the opulence of many would never have been dreamed of, nor could we have had those noble merchant princes whose charities fill all hearts with gratitude and thankfulness to the Bestower of all good, who enabled them, out of the surplus of production over man's consumption, to supply the deficiencies of years of want, and to make cheerful the firesides of many who, though equally deserving, were less fortunate.

LEGAL TENDER.

In my investigations with an eye to the cheapening of the legal tender or circulating medium to the country, it is my duty to examine both sides of the question, in order to arrive at just conclusions, being well aware of the intricate and subtle nature of a subject which has occupied the attention of the profoundest thinkers of our race; more especially as a large percentage of the savings from industry and economy depends on the direction of their investment.

One of the strongest objections that will be urged to a legal tender circulating medium convertible only into a four per cent. gold-bearing bond having twenty years to run, is that it will not command gold at the face on demand. The gold-bearing consols of England have no fixed value in the market, but are governed entirely by the ruling rate of interest and the demand for capital to be used in the enterprises of commerce.

If you wish to change your investment, you must submit to the inexorable law governing all other values. If you sell at 99, 100, or 101, it is only an evidence that you have been offered an investment yielding more than four per cent. per annum.

This is the capitalist's view of the sale and conversion. But if you are a *bull* or a *bear*, the profit or loss will be indicated when it is known which side of the fence you are on, the results of which should have no more effect on the value of a United States bond than the moon has on a Western cheese-factory. After all, it is but the comparison of the income and security of what you are going out of with those of what you are going into. If the securities be equal, the indication is only a change in the rates of interest. So long as the government pays promptly the stipulated rate of interest, and shows ability to retire the loan in full at maturity, no more can be asked: this is all that was promised. The daily fluctuations should give her less concern than the amount of production, and the prosperity of trade, to whose surplus alone can she look for the means of making good her promise.

The next objection is, that our legal tender is not the same as that recognized by the countries intimately connected with us in the exchange of commodities. We have now no circulating medium in common with any other country. Nevertheless, commerce feels not the want. The country was never more prosperous, never accumulated wealth with greater rapidity: all are now merchant princes, and there is no want or destitution throughout the land that a neighbor has not the ability and the disposition to mitigate. What more can be desired? Our annual productions command, the world over, all we want of necessaries and of luxuries, and have filled our national treasury to overflowing.

If England owes her security to a national debt, why should not our national debt become in like manner a security, and at the same time supply a medium that is as necessary to the exchange of commodities as those commodities themselves are to the prosperity of our people? The daily fluctuations in the prices of our bonds need give the government no concern, if she is fully prepared to make good her engagements: the fluctuations can but indicate a change in rates of interest incident to investments springing up at the moment. The conversion of bonds into legal tender will but indicate an increase of productions, or a greater disposition to trade and to liquidate past transactions,—which certainly cannot be objected to, as it is indicative of financial prosperity.

Should the bonds be returned to us from Europe to be converted into gold, the circulating medium of the country would be affected by it no more than it would be by their conversion into mess-pork or any other surplus commodity in the land. With provisions left, we can still command labor, the products of which will bring back all the gold we may desire. It will not be returned until we offer inducements in trade greater than the demand that prompted the conversion of the bonds. The indication would be that gold was more valuable in Europe than with us, and that the people there were short of commodities they could not do without, and were forced to convert their securities into something that might command them from others. The reaction would come in good time, and our productions would force the return, at *our price*, of all we should want, even were it gold.

If we would but rid ourselves of this infatuation for gold, and dispense with it as a circulating medium, it would not be long before the export of provisions in a time of scarcity would bring great tribulation in the land. The interdiction of such export on the part of government, would indicate much more good sense and consideration for its people than were manifested by the European governments during the past century in their edicts against the trade and exportation of the precious metal. This fallacy in regard to gold has happily exploded, and we may hope that the contingency will never rise in which we cannot spare provisions to the needy.

DIVORCEMENT OF GOLD FROM CIRCULATING MEDIUM.

If the circulating medium of a country be a desirable article for export in the purchase of imports, there will necessarily be sudden and ruinous fluctuations in the interior exchanges of the country. The greater the export demand becomes, the more intense will be the monetary pressure and the higher the rate of interest at all the great commercial centers. Depressing and ruinous fluctuations in the prices of all export articles will follow, resulting in losses not only to the producer, but to all speculators. Of all things it is most desirable that the volume of the circulating medium to be used in the transfer of the products of a country should remain as near as possible the same, with liberty to rise and fall with increased production. The rate of interest will be the principal difficulty with which the trader will have to contend in the transfer of the surplus products to market. The rate of interest will be low when the exchange has been effected, or in case of short production, and will rise with abundant production. When the latter is the case we can the better afford to pay usurious rates of interest. Not so, however, if the precious metals form the circulating medium. Being in demand by all nations for their surplus, the exportation of them will soon act in an accelerating ratio, producing in a short time contractions in all departments, resulting in ruinous losses to the producer and trader, and seldom realizing for the capitalist an average rate of interest. All are familiar with the periodical trials of the commercial world. If possible, let them be confined to the trader; he has but little to contend with that is beyond his control. Not so with the producer: his risks are not insurable, and cannot be guarded against by any foresight.

To work this desirable change and protect the circulating medium from the discouraging effects of periodical and speculative influences, and at the same time to bring the surplus of the interior into competition with gold and silver for exportation, let the government, which has the power to regulate the currency and values, give the country a circulating medium equal to the wants of commerce,—say *legal tenders*, not, as at present, payable in gold and silver, but based on the promise that she will, on the funding of her circulating notes, give a bond bearing a certain interest, due at a fixed time,—twenty or thirty years; or let her give a perpetual annuity to the holder, and convert these bonds into legal tenders when called on,—the promise made in the bond for principal and interest to be that of their payment in gold and silver.

This system, with facility of conversion and reconversion at all the commercial centers, would profit not only the government but the capitalist,—the former, in the relief from interest on circulating notes; the latter, whenever he had a surplus of circulating notes,—a certain and easy rate of interest and an easy mode of investment, one, too, which he could easily go out of if the increased productions of the country demanded a larger volume of circulating notes. Rid us of the national bank system and let the entire circulation be legal tenders, and one-half of my proposition will have been carried out. Many advantages will grow out of this divorcement of money of account from an article of merchandise,—each will ebb and flow with supply and demand. All circulating mediums are a tax on a country equal to the average rate of interest. If $700,000,000 be necessary to effect the transfer of produce and the financial exchange of the country, the interest on this sum will be gained by the government. This of itself will be equal to a reduction of one-fourth of the interest on our entire debt, and will withdraw a like sum of bonds from market,—effecting an improvement in all credits. There will be a double demand for bonds;—on the one hand, from their drawing a certain interest; on the other, from increase in the circulation. In order to have nothing compulsory in this arrangement, the conversion of bonds into *legal tenders*, and *vice versa*, should be at the market rate. This will be influenced principally by the ruling rate of interest growing out of supply and demand. Our indebtedness and promises would then differ very little from those of England. All that is promised to the holder is interest at five per cent. per annum. The conversion and reconversion on the part of the government and of her people is a daily business. The fluctuations in the price of gold or of produce do not give the government much concern, except when she has to buy or sell as an individual. The Bank of England looks to the supply of gold to meet the wants of commerce, and gives the country the circulating medium to effect the internal exchanges. The government has only to provide what she promises the holder of her obligations—gold for interest; and when her income is larger than her payments, the surplus is invested in her consols at the market rate.

PRODUCTION AND CONSUMPTION.

Production in excess of consumption will bring into the country a surplus. This can only be increased by stimulus to the former and economy in the latter. The larger the accumulation, the greater will be the ability and the greater the willingness on the part of the people to respond to a tax equal to an honorable maintenance of credit. Without the ability or surplus to draw from, it is idle to talk of payment, either of principal or interest. If there be not an annual balance of profit throughout the land, apathy and indifference will soon be followed by repudiation, rather than allow the springs that give life to enterprise to dry up. Men will fold their arms and look with stoic indifference on a tottering public credit when their fortunes are gradually melting away under the influence of an overburdening tax, not only on the homestead but on the energies of the people.

Schemes and palliatives are but temporary expedients to gain time, and in the end will bring ruin on all interested. Far better is it to make an honest showing and pay what you can, in case an extension will bring no improvement of fortune.

It is not the financier or the man of expedients who is needed at the helm: their day passed away with the rebellion. We now have to come down to matter-of-fact actual payment. The man who will remove restrictions upon commerce, stimulate production, and inaugurate a steady system of liquidation, is the man we want now. Give us less political jobbing, and let rigid economy be exercised in the collection and disbursement of our immense resources. The happy influence will soon reach the producer, and ere long he, too, will find his annual surplus increasing; from which he will the more cheerfully meet the demands of the tax-gatherer.

It is worse than useless to consume our time in seeking palliatives and in tinkering to keep up the public credit. Strike deep at the root; show ability to pay; let the annual surplus in the country be large and increasing, and ere long the balance of trade—the great commercial barometer—will bring the wished-for credit. We may legislate and re-legislate, may resort to one expedient after another, but in the end all will prove worthless if we are destitute of thrift and economy; give to the country this leverage power and the security of a continuance, and in a few years the obligations of the government will be at par with gold. The promise of the government, bearing three or four per cent. interest, will bring into the country any commodity we want, and, with a universal surplus, a sufficiency of the great *bugbear*, gold.

When I undertook this investigation, it was in the hope that in time I might be able to demonstrate a great truth underlying production, consumption, and the laws governing exchange by and through a medium. No part of the investigation will be found to favor the acquisition of wealth except through industry and economy. I have not been at war with any party, sect, or system, nor have I been working for any other end than the development of truth. If the establishment of the principle should overthrow other views or systems, all I can say is, let truth prevail, and let error be discarded as far as lies in the power of weak, erring mortals.

I believed there was an elementary principle which, if by analysis it could be made manifest in the exchange of products, would insure to labor the just reward of honest toil and place in each field of enterprise an unalterable and just medium to be used in the exchange of its products. Finding all mediums to be conventional, I could see no justice in delegating to any production or article of merchandise the arbitrary power of fixing the value of all others, and especially to the one so pre-eminently migratory in its habits and artful in its concealments, that at the words "presto, change," it vanishes from human sight. It is the little "joker" and three thimbles; when you see it placed under one, and bet on it, you find it is not there.

As produce measures and buys produce, all commodities should have a fair chance, and no monopoly should be given to one product over another. If I desire your surplus more than you do mine, give me an inducement in quantity; but do not tell me that yours is worth more than mine because yours can be used as a legal tender. If you did not give it additional value, how can you honestly lay claim to the difference? If government and law have given you this power over me, is it not unneighborly to use it to the ruin of myself and family, when I exercise industry and economy? And these I must have exercised, or else I should not have the necessaries and conveniences of life and a house for shelter. But, because I have had the misfortune to promise it you as a legal tender, you will force me to obtain it, at whatever sacrifice to myself.

The conclusion is that productions should have a fair field and be the measure of each other. When I give an order or bill of exchange for a value, however large the amount may be, the paper on which it is written has no value in itself, but it caused the delivery of the goods. A circulating medium can do no more; but it can do all this, even though it be as worthless as the paper on which the bill of exchange was written.

To clothe a medium of paper with this power, the issue must be controlled by the necessity that called it into being. No party can be so competent to judge of the supply as those who have the sole interest, and that is the people of this country. If they go to the government and say, "We have your bonds bearing four per cent. per annum interest in gold," and offer to rid it of the tax, preferring, as they may do, mess-pork to gold, and ask for legal-tender notes, it is the duty and the interest of the government to issue them. It is the people desiring to use their own notes in the transfer and circulation of their property. The fact that they have been able to give a valuable consideration (a gold bond) is conclusive, and should be evidence to all interested parties that they are able to make good this promise at their convenience; and if misfortune should ever overtake them collectively, their losses will be confined to themselves and not visited on parties having no direct. interest in the matter. The losses, if any, will be distributed as equitably as any system of bankruptcy could devise. We will still have our country and the assets that may be left.

Now, you will naturally inquire, What will be the effect if all Europe should throw its bonds on the market and take up the circulating legal-tender notes and hold them from circulation? For a moment it will depress the prices of all commodities, inducing the purchasers of bonds and the banking institutions at once to turn them and their reserve into a medium in order to buy up the values in the country: in this state of the market, if the European holders of the notes should wish to realize and throw on the market the additional quantity of circulating medium, the country will have gained, from the enhanced prices of their products and property, all that it had previously lost,—enabling many citizens to reinvest in bonds (or fund the notes). One great security against such violent changes will be that our banking institutions will have made discounts and loans from the accumulation of deposits, and will be compelled to furnish legal tenders to their customers and depositors. This will cause them to keep at all times their reserve in bonds, in order that they can at any moment meet the demand for circulating notes. At this point (in order to meet the next inquiry), it may be stated that a system of banking on values without circulating notes will be inaugurated, realizing for them and all parties interested larger and surer profits than have ever been realized by any or all the banking schemes ever inaugurated in this country—not excepting the present national banks, with all the monopoly and prestige of government indorsements and double interest.

It is only necessary to refer to the banking establishments in London, and the enormous profits realized, to see at a glance the effect of banking when freed from the uncertain contingencies of the issue of circulating notes that so often drive them and the country to bankruptcy. These banks transact all their business by the use of Bank of England notes, checks, bills of exchange, etc. The banks referred to are the following:

	Capital.	Deposits.
London and Westminster	$5,000,000	$75,000,000
Union	3,500,000	80,000,000
London Joint Stock	3,000,000	70,000,000
Aggregate.	$11,500,000	$225,000,000

Their average annual dividends are thirty per cent. per annum, or fifteen per cent. every six months. Now, compare this with the Bank of England,—the great regulator of the measure of exchange, provider of the legal tender, and fiscal agent of the government, whose notes are received and disbursed for all public dues,—which, with a capital of some $70,000,000, has a deposit, both public and private, of only an average of about $100,000,000, and a circulation of about $100,000,000, from all which she earns and declares dividends of not more than six and a half per cent. per annum. What makes this great difference in the sum of profits? The Bank of England has the *bag* to hold for all parties, and her circulating notes subject her to all the vibrations and vagaries of gold seeking more profitable and distant markets, forcing her, whenever in peril and trouble, to call on the government for aid and protection from pressure within and without.

Now, I would have all parties to hold their own *bags* and take their grists to none but *Uncle Sam's mill*, where they can *toll* it, and, if they make a mistake, will have no one to blame but themselves, and will have the satisfaction of knowing, when returning home, that the overplus is in the great government *bin*, laid up for the day of need.

If the produce of a country will not buy commodities, then it should not receive or give credit.

If a country needs a legal tender more than goods, it is doing the producers a service not to place their wants with the wants of those seeking a legal tender.

If you want a legal tender to the full value of your produce, you do not want calico. You must do without one or the other; and if you have nothing to exchange you must do without both, and go to work to get something to gratify your wants, if you have any. Honest labor will always find capital willing to furnish the necessaries to sustain it while at work.

A circulating medium being necessary in the disposal of commodities, and a convenience worth some price, which can be measured only by the value in use, the power that issues it should be paid a reasonable consideration. If the rate of interest the issuing power is willing to pay be four per cent. per annum for the use of a legal tender or money of account, it is but reasonable that the government (being the people) should be paid this sum for the use. Now, if you desire this medium to such a degree that you are willing to pay more than four per cent., and will surrender to the government her obligation calling for this rate, four per cent., in exchange for the legal tender, then you will have paid the price or worth of the medium or convenience.

It is the duty of the government to establish light-houses and to undergo many other charges for the protection of the lives and property of her citizens; it is not less her duty to furnish, in financial matters, the head-light and guide to all her citizens who are willing and able to pay for it, and not expose them to the liability of being deceived by the false lights of others in so delicate a matter as the disposal of the products of their labor.

As the design is to protect all rights without undue bias in favor of any, in giving to the people this legal tender and measure of value, there should be a universal standard by which it could be measured, and this currency or medium should be obtainable only in one way,—in exchange for four per cent. bonds having thirty years to run to maturity. I would have the rule so rigid that gold, the ultimate measure, could not command these circulating notes and measure of value. A party having gold or mess-pork, and desiring to convert them into legal tender, should be compelled to convert them into four per cent. bonds, and these alone should be able to command them. A firm adherence to this would give all parties an equitable chance in a free market to supply their wants at market prices. With four per cent. bonds for circulating medium and legal tender, all commodities and evidences of debt would compete for bonds or legal tender,— the demand adjusting the supply, and the supply fixing the demand. Bonds would then be rated by the value of legal tender, and the circulating medium would be regulated by the amount of productions it would command. All commodities would then measure each other,—and the medium used in exchanging them, having no intrinsic value while so used, would be estimated by its use and convenience in facilitating the sale and purchase of production and the liquidation of debt.

The capitalist, or lender of the legal tender or medium, only gives the command in the market of legal-tender value, or so much of production; and if he receives back at the stipulated time a similar order for commodities, and his four, six, or ten per cent. for the use, there can be no injustice; for I hold that a legal tender of to-day that is fixed to remain and be the same forever, is no more likely to depreciate than the productions it was originally exchanged for. An order for gold itself is no more likely to purchase a greater quantity of mess-pork than the mess-pork is to buy a greater quantity of gold. The value of one is found by what it will exchange for; the other may have an indispensable value in sustaining human labor during the production of articles in greater demand.

It is the fear of depreciation in the legal tender that deters governments from a change from gold as a standard. It is in their power to render the one as unchangeable as the other, if they will but be honest and limit the procurement of the medium in exchange only for a fixed value, and let it be the limiting power of the value of the medium. If there should for a time be more on the market than the wants of trade demand, the excess will soon find its way back to bonds; and if there should be more bonds on the market than there is capital to bear, then it is the misfortune of the holders. In this state of the market it would be the duty of the government to provide for the redemption of the portion in excess of the demand, at the fixed rate of interest. This, however, can never take place so long as there are articles of value to exchange. In this case holders of bonds can readily part with them and go into investments paying higher rates of interest. It is impossible for any securities or commodities to escape the great law of trade, of being measured by each other, and not by any one standard. The standard or legal tender is only the limiting power of debt; and to find out the value of the debt, you must compare the legal tender with the necessaries, conveniences, and amusements it will command. The circulating medium of a country must be viewed in the light of a great highway to market, that can be used and traveled over by thousands who own none of the stock, but who must finally pay such toll as will eventually give a dividend to the owners, or else the road will not be renewed and kept in good order. This being the case, it is no part of the business of the government to undertake at the end of the line to deliver any other commodities to the consignee than the particular goods shipped. If parties demand gold instead of mess-pork, or flour in place of gold, it will be her duty to turn to the bill of lading and discharge the cargo in the order and condition in which it was received.

CREDIT THROUGH CIRCULATING NOTES.

I DOUBT much whether credit, through a circulating medium or bank-notes not legal tender, ever conferred any real substantial benefit on the productions of any country, from the fact that it does not create or call into being any of the necessaries or conveniences of labor. Gold can be sent off to distant countries and there command the tools and implements of reproduction; but banknotes, even if convertible into gold, and of high credit, will not circulate as money in other countries. Now, we all know that the moment conversion is demanded in order to get a commodity for export, the loan will be denied. Banks of circulation desiring credit do not lend gold; but for a percentage they will undertake to lend credit, or indorse you up to the country, by involving your friends, in the shape of notes payable on demand, to be exchanged for your neighbor's produce and supplies. If you are industrious and economical, in nine cases out of ten you can procure the supplies from your neighbor direct, and need not complicate the entire industry of the country by giving to a numerous horde of wild speculators a fiction with which they can buy up the commodities needed so much by the labor of the country. The instances of prudence, or of the use of economy, in the issuing of these credits, have been so rare, that I am firmly convinced a greater degree of prosperity would have been developed throughout the country, by confining all credit direct to values, and their use to the prudent and industrious: the revulsions then would not only have been few, but would have been confined to the adventurer. There is already too much credit given in the sale of the products of labor. If the holders of values would demand values in exchange, losses would not be a *wipe-out*, but would be only for the percentage of depreciation. Confine all time sales and purchases to bulls and bears, and let them settle their own differences, if able. The country will then have something better than promises in return for the products of human labor. If there remain a surplus in the country, industry will be able to command it in exchange for an honest day's work. Should there still be left commodities over consumption, they will command the surplus of others without this continual speculation on credit, and its abuse. Traders will spring up, with the requisite facilities to seek new and increasing markets. Without this annual surplus, the food of commerce, those engaged in the exchange cannot prosper or become opulent.

If properly considered, there can be no loan of capital in the exchange of products, they being themselves *the capital*. Confine the speculator to values in exchange for values, and you will have less use for a bankrupt court. Give to labor a fair advance on the prospective products, and they in their turn will command the necessaries, conveniences, and amusements of life. The supply is much more likely to continue equal to the demand than if allowed to be dissipated by the reckless speculator devoid of capital other than his wits.

I am not at war with credit, nor do I wish to lessen its beneficial influences; but as it can be, and continues to be, abused, my desire is to lessen or mitigate its evils. I am well aware that my limited ability has caused many of my statements and arguments to be somewhat difficult of comprehension; but, at the same time, I do not underrate my efforts so far as not to feel sure of the enlightenment of a majority of those who will take the trouble to think of what I have undertaken to demonstrate.

But few are fond of investigations so intricate as the foregoing, and I can only urge on this class the obligation due to themselves and their country to make themselves better informed in regard to many of the mysteries and truths involved in the ever-widening and extended commerce growing out of the industry and economy of a go-ahead people such as we are, whose annual production and consumption have never been equaled by the most favored nation.

To the aged and the man of leisure, I trust I have rendered needless the intense thought which it is absolutely necessary to bring to bear in all such investigations, and have enabled them to pursue the subject to a more enlightened conclusion.

Many passages will be found to be a seeming repetition; but the subject is so subtle that I was compelled to approach the underlying principles from different stand-points, in order to shed more light on the main question. Hence the many expressions and verifications of the same truths; and I trust the unfamiliar reader will pardon the seeming tautology, especially if it has given him a clear understanding of the unchangeable truths of political economy.

MEDIUM SHOULD BE LEGAL TENDER.

IF labor be the first cost of all value, then an abundance or large production will cheapen prices when compared with all other commodities not so found; in other words, more of the increased production, in the absence of an increased demand, **must be given** for values that have not changed in quantity or for which the demand has not increased. Now, should the position of the markets to-day be three barrels of flour for one of mess-pork, the same proportions will exist in the future, provided the supply and demand continue unchanged; this rule will be found equally applicable to all productions of present necessity, but cannot be applied so invariably to articles of luxury; they must continue to fluctuate with the ability or surplus of those who have heretofore indulged in them. Disastrous ventures in trade, from whatever cause, will cut short the power to indulge, especially of that class which was accustomed to take the largest amount of luxuries: the labor producing these luxuries may, from want of demand, be thrown on that class producing the necessaries of life, or that portion of labor which sustains the labor of all other occupations. The effect will be an increase of products of prime necessity, a cheapening of the money price of labor, and an abridgment of the consumption of luxuries by the parties consuming most largely, cheapening them for a time, and then extension to those who previously shared but sparingly, but in the end (from the enhanced price consequent upon the withdrawal of labor) a total depreciation. Undue speculations and unguarded ventures bring trouble and disaster on all parties. Production may be ill assisted and cause great embarrassment and want for a time, but no degree of general prosperity can bring an oversupply or glut. An increase in productions gives greater ability to buy; and the buyer's ability to consume enables the party making the exchange with him to dispose of his wares and increase his consumption, satisfying the great law of production, the stimulus of which is the desire to consume. So long as there is a general surplus there will be no impediment to the consumption. In this connection arises the great necessity of discouraging all wild speculations by forbidding the use of any device that will either decoy or deceive labor, the result of which is to estrange capital from labor, and cause the one to be shy of the other. It is the products of last year that put labor in motion; but without the co-operation of capital—the tools and labor-saving machines of the present day—the needful conveniences of an economical existence could with difficulty be procured. No human labor could compete with the mowing machinery in haymaking, or with the reaper in furnishing cheap grain; while the rail-splitter, with his old-fashioned axe, would be far behind the one using the improved Collins. All this goes to prove that there is a continuous copartnership between capital and labor; each is working for a share of the crop. In agriculture, frequently, both share alike; but where the preponderance of capital in machinery, etc. is great, labor must be contented with a smaller percentage. There must be harmony, liberality, and fair dealing; the one must not stipulate for the lion's share, nor must the other be wanting in an honest effort to fulfill the contract. No extended commerce or trade can spring into existence without these requisites,—each interest should be shielded from the disasters of the reckless speculator and gambler in values.

Capital is the great benefactor of labor, saving up by economy its surplus, and sharing its fruits with industry and reproduction. It makes no difference in the relationship of capital to labor, whether the owner of it puts labor in motion, or whether the retired capitalist lends it to an intermediate agent. Still, labor, if honestly dealt with, must have the accustomed reward for its toil, leaving the remainder of the products to be apportioned between capital and the agent. The intermediate man is the speculator on credit, working for the difference: he may be overreached and bring disaster. Capital may survive the loss with but little inconvenience, as its eggs are not generally all put in one basket; but let there be no device in all these exchanges and complications to deprive labor of its full share, for the Good Book says, "the laborer is worthy of his hire." The customary devices used by this intermediate agent to force success against an advanced demand, are circulating notes, or orders for capital carrying the promise of legal tender: when these are dishonored, the loss falls entirely on capital and labor. The latter may not survive the loss, no portion of which can fall on the speculator. He may be inconvenienced and embarrassed by being thrown out of the ring, but the only capital he put into the business was capacity; while in, he received his grub, and he retires without profit.

Still, this intermediate agent is not only useful but absolutely necessary in the extension of the intercourse between capital and labor, and, if he had not been enabled to borrow, in addition to capital, these false orders, or bank-notes, *so called*, he might have been induced, in due time, to discontinue the venture and save all parties from loss. Both capital and labor would have had no other inconvenience or loss than the looking up of a more profitable employment. Do not give to the middle man, or agent, the power to consume capital, or to rob the laborer; if you do, capital may charge all the losses on labor, which may have been honest in effect, but badly directed. The less intervention of credit there is between capital and labor, the better for both: the one is endeavoring to encourage industry, the other to give an honest increase, while credit is a two-edged sword going between. Capital must not be allowed to become enervated and indolent; it must learn the importance of infusing into its offspring the economy that gave it birth, by a proper training in youth; and a familiarity in the handling of the tools used by labor will guard against many cuts. It is the want of this early training that brings industry and economy into bad repute, and which in time will dissipate the accumulations of thrift and economy.

I would cause to be studied by all the youths of the land, as their first lesson in political economy, the unchangeable law, first promulgated by Adam Smith, that "Labor was the first price, the original purchase-money, paid for all things. It was not by gold or silver, but by labor, that all the wealth of the world was originally purchased, and its value to those who possess it, and to those who want to exchange it for some new production, is precisely equal to the quantity of labor which it enables them to purchase."

Low money prices are generally interpreted to mean hard times and a want of prosperity; but the reverse is oftener the truth. Large productions are the sure indications of thrifty and favorable harvest, and invariably bring low money values. There can be no better evidence of industry and the reward of the husbandman than abundance; the cry of hard times and inadequate reward of labor can be traced to the too free use of credit, which unfortunately remains the same, however low the prices may rule for large productions. If the money-price or legal tender required be also an article of merchandise, and be not present with the abundance of commodities, its value will be enhanced, while the surplus of other productions seeking a market must sink to a speculative point in order to induce the importation of this commodity (legal tender); then labor, that has promised a portion of its earnings, or their value, in another or defunct commodity, cannot liquidate with a comparative *show* of equity; the tendency is to discourage industry and cripple commerce and increase in a twofold manner, first by discouragement, and then by a want of the usual surplus, to perpetuate the business of exchange and trade.

From the best data that have been obtained, the circulating medium of a country is equal in value to about one-fifth of the annual productions. Then three thousand millions of productions will require six hundred millions to effect the exchanges and liquidate debt, costing the citizens thirty-six millions annually, or six per cent. interest, this being the lowest estimate that can be placed on it. Now, this is one and one-fifth per cent. on the entire annual productions of the interior country. A portion of this tax must be paid by every man, woman, and child that enters the market with goods for sale or debt contracted for goods exchanged. If one-half of the products are consumed by the producer, the tax on the remainder will be, say two and a half per cent., or equal to the usual commission for the sale of raw products; that is, equal to fifty cents per barrel on pork and twenty cents on flour. As all this tax is on that portion of commodities to be exchanged before consumption, it is peculiarly onerous on those who make nothing for home consumption: that portion of commodities consumed at the place of production pays no part of the charge for a medium, but only that portion convertible by the medium.

The above charge for a medium is confined to the internal affairs of the country, and is to be borne by its exchangeable products. That portion of commodities for export, to be used in the purchase of imports, has, in addition to its quota of the domestic charges, a new set of its own, growing out of its circulating medium, bills of exchange, and that portion of the tax required to keep up a reserve of gold to be used when called on to liquidate balances, custom-house dues, and other charges incident to the sale and conversion into other commodities, or goods for home consumption: all these, when summed up, amount to no inconsiderable sum,—at times so large that the entire value of the venture is consumed, to the discouragement of further production.

The reserve of gold necessary to insure an uninterrupted export and import trade cannot well be estimated at less than one-fourth the exports, say $100,000,000. The interest at six per cent. on this sum, or $6,000,000, is equal to one and a half per cent. on $400,000,000. In the case of a gold circulating medium, to be used in the interior of a country as its only legal tender, you force these export commodities to keep up the circuit of the entire medium of the country, when it really amounts to only a portion of the products to be exchanged; while a well-regulated internal legal-tender circulating medium, such as I have been advocating, would save to the exports of the country all charges except its own, freeing them from the additional charge of not less than five per cent. for hunting up a gold medium when it is not in sight, but absent at some distant point, where, in all probability, it is profitably employed, and, to cause its withdrawal, we must offer large inducements and sacrifices on our exportable commodities.

I will now endeavor to show that production is still worse off. With a bank-note medium convertible into a legal tender gold, we will still place the needs at $600,000,000 for a circulating medium, and allow the banks, as usual, to issue three to one, or hold in reserve $200,000,000. Now, I contend that the people are paying six per cent. at least on this $600,000,000, and losing the use of

$200,000,000 of gold in sustaining the bank-note medium; all this is to keep them from suspension, which, nevertheless, we all know will periodically occur, and the losses from which cannot be estimated at less than thirty-three and one-third per cent. every ten years, two and a half per cent. per annum on the entire paper circulation.

Let us make a summary of the charges and losses incident to a gold circulating medium and legal tender for interior and foreign commerce: $600,000,000 at six per cent. interest is $36,000,000; $200,000,000 for foreign trade, $12,000,000; five per cent. on $500,000,000, $25,000,000; $73,000,000; two and a half per cent. per annum, loss on a convertible bank-note medium, $15,000,000; annual loss incident to internal and external trade, $88,000,000. Now, I contend that with a legal-tender medium, such as we have indicated in the foregoing, $100,000,000 in a gold reserve will be amply sufficient to take care of all the charges incident to the exports of $400,000,000 and imports of $400,000,000. This is only a running, constant charge, and would give a credit of $6,000,000 on the $88,000,000, leaving a net charge saved to the industry of the country of $82,000,000, nearly equal to twenty per cent. on the entire export trade, or five per cent. on the internal and external exchanges of all the commodities of the country seeking a market.

In searching for the great truth underlying the prosperity of our country, and the adoption of it on the exchanges necessary to bring an abundance for consumption out of a reinvigorated production, I have been compelled to weigh and verify the charges surrounding the entire subject, and can the more readily give the foregoing as *at least* a near approximation to the loss incident to the labor and industry of man. This large sum will be found equal to the charges on one-half of our bonded debt, and might serve as the nucleus of a sinking fund that in a reasonable time, with demands of a legal-tender medium, would "wipe out the whole" and leave the country prosperous and its internal trade uninterrupted by the disturbing influences incident to all circulating mediums, if of merchandise, realizing to the country the value of the great truth which I asserted at the beginning of this book, and freeing itself from the *curse* that must follow in the track of error.

One fruitful source of all our troubles and want of thrift from the use of bank-notes as a circulating medium, grows out of the periodical pressure on the issues for payment, causing the owners and holders of values to withdraw them from use, for fear of loss if trusted to the varying fortunes of the speculator on credits. So long as these values, whether of gold, pork, or flour, are withheld from circulation or reproduction, all the natural increase to the country has been lost. Give to capital the necessaries and conveniences of labor, confidence through a uniform and unchangeable system of security, and all will be made available in reproduction. No loss will be incident to hoarding or *hiding*. If there be those fearful to credit themselves, let us not quarrel with them,—they are the storekeepers of misfortunes and universal want by the hoarding up of the surplus products of the imprudent,—they are a portion of the great machinery of life, without which there would be times when there would be no oil to grease the parts. Let us be charitable and magnanimous, and concede them their day; it is to be hoped their reign may be short, but let it have all the *éclat* due to this long obscurity and want of consideration by the mass.

There has been and continues to be much speculation as to how our large debt can be paid. Many think, or say without thinking, that it can, if we have ability, be done at once or *immediately*. I admit we could cancel the debt if some unseen power, such as Aladdin's wonderful lamp, would place us in possession of the legal tender *gold* to this large amount; but the very application of the money to this purpose would bring about such a revulsion in the value of gold that, from its redundancy, thousands would become bankrupt, and many of the holders of the bonds would be brought to the verge of starvation.

Gold may be by law a legal tender for debt, but cannot be made to command other values if, from abundance, it should lose its value. Now we will take the reverse of the picture. Suppose this wonderful lamp, or unseen power, should place us in possession of the requisite amount of pork, flour, and other commodities to discharge this debt at the present gold prices for the same; do you suppose it would command the gold to an amount which would pay even the interest for one or two years?

Both these positions are strictly in accord with the laws of value; in the first case of gold, the injustice would be unpardonable, and in the second, the pork, flour, etc. would become so worthless, for want of a legitimate demand, that but little of the debt would be discharged.

Now, as nature has not placed it in our power to make a *coup d'état*, we will conform to her laws and have a due regard to consumption and the wants of mankind,—not undertake to force sales on the one hand or be unjust on the other; but there is one thing we can do, without fear of censure from the creditors, in favor of the debtor, and that is, do nothing that will appreciate gold; do not use it as a circulating medium and legal tender, nor hoard it up from use; when you have it, throw it on the market and let it seek investments,—it will then have a chance to be returned to us probably at a lower comparative value in exchange for our commodities.

If one or two other large competitors for gold as a medium should discard it as such, it may bring about such a state of things that the same amount of mess-pork, flour, etc. received for the bonds will call them in and cancel the debt. This state of the market will satisfy that portion of our citizens who contend that we did not receive value for the bonds when they were issued. I am not of that class, and think that, when all the circumstances surrounding them are weighed, a different opinion will prevail.

In 1862, when the legal-tender act was passed, the creditor portion of the country had to receive their collections in the redundant depreciated medium. It was from this class alone, holding the floating capital, that purchasers for the bonds could be expected, and, as they paid *par* for them, they were compelled to return the value fixed on them for debts due them in gold.

There was nothing wrong in all this on either side,—the necessity of the government was paramount to all considerations of propriety or justice, and the capitalist had to protect himself in the best way he could, which was by the exchange of a due debt paid in legal tender for a bond bearing on the future good fortunes of the country; they are now coming around to value received and an adjustment of the account on the square. It is but the verification of the old adage: "What goes over the devil's back will come under his belly."

LEGAL TENDER ONLY TO BE ISSUED FOR BONDS.

If the position I have taken became the policy of the government in giving to the interior an independent circulating medium and legal tender in exchange for four per cent. bonds, as I stated previously, no power should be delegated to the issuing department to go beyond this, nor give to the country one dollar in exchange for anything else, not even gold. Why should this article of merchandise be dignified with the power of speculation, and mess-pork, flour, or any other commodity in universal demand, not be admitted to the same privilege? If this standard of value or medium of exchange is intended to measure all values and credit, and be a legal tender, no commodity can take its place and be a reliable measure. The moment you allow this medium to be issued in exchange for any production, you have completed the exchanges, and the tendency is to debase the legal standard by instituting a rivalry between commodities. The principle I am contending for excludes any commodity from becoming a legal tender or measure.

It certainly looks very flattering and tempting to have gold offered in exchange for the medium or legal tender, from the fact of its easy conversion into all other productions of all countries and nations. With me this is one of the very reasons that would cause me to exclude it. If you connect it by deposit with the issuing power, you at once lock it up and deprive reproduction of all the profits and benefits that might have been derived from its conversion into valuable implements for the extension of production, or deprive consumption of one of its stimulants to renewed exertion. I readily admit there would be no deterioration in bulk, such as would be the case if the exchange had been for mess-pork, from the fact of its liability to decay; but it would be less liable to the designs of thieves and rogues.

You may now ask, What is to be done with the excess of gold when it has ceased to be used as a medium of exchange? I answer, Convert it, like all other commodities, and if you have a surplus over, unemployed, buy our bonds, which will help to cheapen the rate of interest. It is the unlocking of values, and bringing them into use, that cheapens them in the market. Hoarding or holding, by withdrawal from sale, tends above all other devices of man to heighten comparative prices and give them an undue influence in the hands of those monopolizing the market.

There is one other serious objection to allowing gold to be exchanged for the circulating medium, and that is the constant comparison of it with the legal tender, and the impossibility of the government getting clear of it without a violation of one of the fundamental principles underlying this entire policy, to wit, the exchange of this gold for her notes. This would be the conversion into gold of all notes on demand, and would bring about the antagonism of principles from which I am laboring to free the country. She certainly could not pay it out to bondholders without doing great injustice to those who had invested in her funded debt, using that which did not belong to her, and contracting a new debt, which would recoil on the holders of the old, from the undue complication with the holders of the circulating medium, by depreciation of the sum previously held, when compared with the amount actually needed to effect the changes of the interior. The true principle is to allow every tub to stand on its own bottom. If any monopolies are permitted, let the government retain them in her own hands for the benefit and use of the people. The consumption or investment of gold, like that of all other commodities, will stimulate production, giving to man all the instruments and devices of labor to aid him in effecting a surplus, from which alone can come ability to pay taxes, and will keep up her revenue to a point that will insure credit and a high degree of prosperity.

No one will deny that if you take away from the factory the motive power, or from the farm the implements of husbandry, you have inflicted on the country and its labor a loss in land and machinery, to the extent of the destruction of all income. Now, I hold that if a government has an article of value which, by a simple exchange, will infuse new life into this machinery and restore to the land its wonted increase, she has inflicted a great wrong on labor—especially if that value is a value only when in use—by locking it up in the vaults of a bank, instead of sending it to the country, where the implements can be purchased to sustain industry, and where that value is in demand.

The government has to make good her promises of gold to the holders of her bonds for interest. Let her go on collecting from customs that portion needed in the liquidation of debt in accordance with the contract; let commerce and trade hunt up such commodities as they desire to deal in and have promised in the payment of balances; let us have no undue influence in the way of the prompt and honorable fulfillment of engagements by all parties in the basis of the original contract, and never legalize any illegitimate competition. Allow the dealers in gold, like those in other commodities, to consult their own interest and convenience in trade and the division of the profits in any values in which they may desire to invest their surplus. If the government undertakes to furnish its people with a medium of exchange and liquidation of balances, we have no claim on her further than the commodities to be exchanged by it. If she has promised us flour, we have no right to demand mess-pork or gold. Before we can have a clear insight into this position, we must separate the medium from the values to be exchanged by it,—the railway and the rolling-stock from the commodities to be transported over the road. There can be no objection to the government receiving gold on deposit and issuing, as at present, certificates. This will give a safe place to those interested in the trade to keep it until commerce may demand its withdrawal, and will save to the import and export trade a large sum in transportation. It certainly would be rendering to the trader a great service and facility in the payment of duties, subjecting him to no other expense than that of a cancellation of certificates.

TRIAL AND SUMMARY.

AFTER a careful review of the foregoing investigations, calling for a change, as I have attempted to show, from error to truth, I deem it just to call a general council of the interests involved, in order that a statement may be made of the defense and argument leading to a final disposition by the highest tribunal.

The government of the United States having called on the following to make their defense, they will be heard in their order:

>The People.
>Gold.
>Domestic Commerce.
>Foreign Commerce.
>Balance of Trade.
>Cotton.
>Mess-Pork.
>Flour.
>General Productions.
>Consumption.
>Fixed Capital.
>Banking.
>Legal Tender.
>Circulating Medium.

UNCLE SAM.—Having been called upon by my people to arbitrate in regard to a final dissolution of the relations hitherto existing between certain productions, and in order to a better understanding, I will first call upon the people to state their case.

The People.—We have lately been pondering over the deductions made by one of our number from what he claims to be a great truth, or an original element underlying all our prosperity. He asserts that "if the circulating medium and legal tender of a country be an article of merchandise desirable for export, you have inflicted a curse instead of a blessing on us," and asks for the disuse of gold as a medium in our domestic transactions, for the reason that productions buy and exchange for productions, the medium being conventional, and having no other value than what we give it by the exchange of our products for it; that our mess-pork will purchase as much flour through a medium having no intrinsic value, without the relations of the two being disturbed by the intervention of a third commodity like gold, arbitrarily fixing the difference when absent or present, and which is well known to be liable to the most violent fluctuations, which often bring wide-spread disaster in their train.

If this be true, and the medium should have no intrinsic value, but merely a relative one, all estimates would begin at zero. The measure would not only be fair, but unchangeable,—0 from pork and pork remains, flour from 0 and 0 remains; all values would then have free orbits confined to supply and demand, and all excesses would gravitate toward the center in comparative value, and would be estimated by their utility. In view of all these facts, and the large amount of mess-pork, flour, and other products we will have to force on foreign countries to purchase the large sum of gold required, say five hundred millions, we will not only be embarrassed, but our ability to make good the maturing obligations you have indorsed for us, which also call for gold, will be lessened. To bring into competition with these engagements so disturbing and enervating a medium as gold, will only give rise to complications, and, as we believe, inflict upon us a *curse*.

To enable us to overcome the many difficulties besetting our path in carrying the large debt now upon our shoulders, we come forward in our sovereign capacity and pledge ourselves jointly and severally to the extinguishment of the last remaining vestige of debt, in the commodity stipulated to be paid, out of our surplus. But in order to do this, we must husband and economize our reserve for reproduction. The medium of exchange being a luxury, and a legal tender a necessity, we ask that you indorse our joint notes to the amount of our gold-bearing bonds, promising that you will exchange these notes for bonds only, and, when desired, will fund them again into a four per cent. gold promise having thirty years to run to maturity; and we pledge ourselves to use them, and no other notes, as a medium in the exchange of our productions, and to receive them as a legal tender for all debts due us. As we now need our five hundred millions for a medium, it will relieve you from the collection of the thirty millions of dollars required to pay the annual tax on the bonds that must be canceled in order to get the legal tender and circulating medium. The rapid development of this great country and the annual increase of our productions will cause a similar and continuous call for these notes. Finally, we enjoin that the only basis for these notes shall be bonds, and that bonds can be issued only on the return of the circulating notes. If you should collect in any one year more gold than is necessary to pay maturing obligations in the shape of interest promises, apply the balance to the extinguishment of the most onerous debt that you have the privilege of canceling.

Gold.—I have listened, without interrupting, to the remarks of the people, and am astonished at their ingratitude and their disposition to rob me of regal power, especially on the part of those who have subjected so much territory to my use and have worshiped me so devotedly. It is but a short time since they set me up as a god and ran me up from a man to fifteen men in buckram suits, because I happened to slay all the bulls and bears in my room, except the small portion that escaped by the side-doors and windows; even some of these were not able to find their way home, and had to be placed in the mad-house. In the morning, all parties agreed that I was worth one hundred and thirty of your dear people, but they declared before three o'clock that I was equal to one hundred and sixty-five, and if it had not been for your untimely interference in tripping me up I do not know what would have been the consequences, nor how near I might have brought your dear people to starvation. I can readily see your drift: you wish to rob me of temporal power, and declare that I am not infallible.

Well, have this as you will, there will be many who will still hoard me up and continue their worship. Though I shall publicly retire from your confidence, no longer to be used by the dirty hands of labor in its daily toil, I shall continue to pass through the hands of the silk-glove gentry, and, before you get to the end of the engagements you have for my use in the future, many hard days' work will have to be performed, and still, as heretofore, many a voyage around the world in search of me may enable me to lead you a wild-goose chase through many a bog and bramble path.

DOMESTIC TRADE.—Give us a medium for our wares that will command the productions of the country, and we will find you a market and bring back calico or any other commodity you desire, even should it be gold. We are disposed to think, after all that has been said by the people, that if they have found a substitute for five hundred millions of dollars, and shall succeed in lessening the annual wants some thirty millions of dollars more, it will deduct a large percentage from the conventional value of gold. Less of their productions will be required to purchase the amount they may need from time to time for any purpose.

FOREIGN TRADE.—We are not alarmed at what your people ask. It will not lessen our profits; but if the change adds to their productions, as it certainly will do, we can sell them more goods and enhance our profits to that extent. There is another feature which appears very favorable, and that is, when we ship your products, we are compelled to go to a banker and dealer in bills of exchange and offer him a draft against the value, and to purchase legal tenders or mediums for the people. We have frequently been greatly inconvenienced and embarrassed, owing to the migratory disposition of gold, in finding the legal tender, and have had to make heavy sacrifices of the productions, to induce the banker to part with the medium; not only this, but we have frequently had our operations limited, when more extended shipments would have paid far better. These difficulties in the sale of exchange are not only a loss to the producer, but affect the home market, from its influence on the foreign, bringing about those sudden fluctuations in prices that are so disastrous to our interest.

COTTON.—One great complaint made by the producers of export articles is, that when the legal tender or gold is absent from the country they are compelled to price all their commodities, or compare them with legal tender, in order to get it, when in fact they only require a small percentage with which to liquidate debt, and might have the balance to exchange for other merchandise, such as pork, flour, etc., which are not influenced to the same extent by the short supply of gold in the country, from the fact that they are consumed in and about home, while I have suffered all the depression from my being an exportable article. If this was all, it might be borne by me, as I have at the present time a sort of monopoly from location, climate, etc. We know the spinners reap no direct advantages from this great loss of ours, but at the same time it is used as a discrimination against our home manufactories, by the cheapening of the exchange used in the purchase of foreign imports. The profit to the dealer in exchange is all that is realized by the country, except where he is also a foreigner; in that case I am paying all the losses, and my people are receiving none of the profits. You may think this difference in exchange that I have paid for a legal tender is a small affair, but the average before the late war was fully five per cent. This on a crop of two hundred millions of dollars is no less than ten millions of dollars which I have been contributing to this despot gold, all of which was used as a discriminating duty against my home factories. Give me my own notes in exchange; they will cancel my debts, pay taxes to you, and realize for me as much mess-pork as they will exchange for, and no questions will be asked as to the value of gold in the purchase of home productions. There are only two questions involved: What is the cost in human labor? and, What is the excess of supply over consumption?

LEGAL TENDER.—During the trying times of the late war I was honored with the position of umpire, liquidator of balances, and medium between you and the products of your people; I was hailed by your soldiers in the field, however disastrous and dangerous the position, as the messenger of good tidings: there was not a commodity in all the land that I could not command. I am well aware that a greater power was delegated to me than justice would have sanctioned, and that I could not honorably undertake to adjust the difference that had been delegated to gold. I made no invidious comparisons with my rival in the settlement of old balances, but passed along as quietly as I could. Although I knew I was growing in appreciation, I made no complaint against the late decision confining me to the times of 1862, or the day of my birth; in this I cheerfully acquiesce, believing it a just decision. The relations between myself and gold are every day becoming more amicable; nevertheless, it will take me some time to forgive and forget that last brick she threw at my head, on the black Friday of September, 1869, although it missed its mark, and dealt some heavy blows among her best friends.

If the power is continued to me as heretofore, I will endeavor not to abuse it nor claim anything more than the people have delegated to me, which is nothing, or zero. I will continue to award as many barrels of flour for one of pork as the state of the market and of supply and demand will permit, and will make no unjust discriminations against gold in any case when it is offered in exchange, especially as we are in need of a considerable quantity of that article to make good our old promises; so long as my people give their surplus productions in exchange for me, I will be to them a faithful medium, and will take no umbrage at their exchanging ten of me for one of flour, or thirty for one of pork. The only indication in that case will be that there has been a failure in the customary yield of grain, and that the cholera has been among the hogs. But should only five dollars be demanded as the value of flour, and fifteen dollars as that of pork, it will be the highest evidence of the smiles of the Giver of all good on industry and labor; and should the bounteous productions ever become as free as air and water, then my measure (zero) will have been reached, and all will hail the millennium. There will no longer be any necessity for my friendly intervention as a medium in the awards to labor or capital, and my career will have ended in triumph.

BALANCE OF TRADE.—So much has already been said and promised that I deem it unnecessary to go further into details. I will only add, keep good faith, and render to me the surplus of productions over consumption which I know industry and economy can call into being. I will undertake to settle all balances, and furnish to your people all the necessaries that may be desired, together with all the gold you may need in the discharge of obligations you have entered into on their behalf.

BANKS.—We rejoice to find that the change is likely to be inaugurated, for we will no longer be called on by the needy, the idle, the dissipated, and the reckless speculator for our notes, to be used in hunting up the surplus products of labor and in risks incident to the clamorous demand for new loans. They have been the source of all our troubles, and caused us to inflict on labor all the heavy burdens incident to the exchange of its products. And when we have been unable to meet all their demands for legal tender, we have been unreasonably set upon and deprived of the provisions we had laid up for the maintenance of our own families. Now that legal tender has undertaken to look up all the surpluses of the country and deposit them with us, to be loaned to and used by industry, and by any others who may give securities for their return, when these values are placed on deposit with us to be used in the development of the country's best interest, we will feel sure not only that they are here, but that they belong to the people. Heretofore, when we gave our orders on the country for its commodities, and they were not in existence, they were immediately returned for gold (a commodity we were generally short of), in order that it might be sent to some other country to insure compliance with the terms of the order. All this, in times of a greater desire to speculate than to produce, coupled with short productions, caused us great uneasiness, and disposed us to think hard of your people. But now, being relieved of this burden of importing and hunting up gold, we feel secure, and for the future will find our interest in the loan of capital to industry. When we look at the small dividends of the Bank of England, some six or eight per cent. per annum, and the large returns (thirty per cent. or more) realized by the banks not called on to issue notes or orders on the country, we feel compelled by self-interest and security to exert our utmost influence in carrying out the wishes of the people. From the above we would by no means have you think we have not made a good thing out of getting interest on your bonds, and your indorsement of our notes free of charge, all of which commanded the values in the country equal with your own notes. But, as we will no longer have to provide this *little joker* gold, we prefer to make our bow and retain our gains.

UNCLE SAM.—I see some disorder and commotion in this hall, occasioned by the unceremonious departure of the idle, the dissipated, the reckless speculator and gambler, and can distinguish such mutterings as, "If there are to be no more wild-cat banks, if all the prizes are to be drawn by industry and economy, and if nothing is promised to those who look to other men's labor and to their own wits for a living, it is time for us to be off, avoiding such unholy combinations against those who by nature have no inclination for work." So soon as order is restored, I will endeavor to sum up the facts and evidence in the case, and give you my opinion and views.

All power is derived from the people; it is to their industry and economy that we are indebted for a surplus of productions over consumption. Without this surplus of the necessaries, conveniences, luxuries, and amusements of life, the bondholders would be unable to fulfill their promises, I would be unable to fulfill mine; and national ruin would ensue.

When the people call into existence this surplus and use it as a legal tender for the extinguishment of contracts, it is the highest evidence that can be given of their honor and integrity. Nor can I see why they should not be suffered to go on and prosper in their own way; no one has any right to heap upon their shoulders unnecessary burdens. If they desire domestic institutions instead of imported ones, they have a right to their preferences, especially if they think the importation of the foreign would introduce a pest, and a continual wrangling. "Let us have peace," whose victories, as the poet says, are no less renowned than those of war. If there be any so wedded to Mammon as to desire gold promises only, there will be no objection.

Foreign exchange has now her own medium (bills of exchange, etc.), which is used not only as a medium but as a legal tender and purchasing power, and she declines having anything to do with the changes contemplated in our internal affairs. Her desire is that surplus commodities shall be exchanged for productions, giving a profit on the inward as well as the outward venture, by which process her gains will be doubled and still greater security given to her operations.

PRODUCTION AND ITS DRAWBACKS.

The leading interest of all countries is production. To increase this, due stimulus must be given to industry, and economy must be infused into every avenue of consumption, that there may be annually an increase of commodities for sale or exchange. Stationary production will soon be overtaken by population, and in years of adversity want and misery will ensue.

Retrograding production tends to force on the

poor decreasing quantities and qualities of food, till at last death comes to their relief. Not so with increasing production: the daily wants of the masses annually expand, and the luxuries of one year become the necessaries of the next, banishing misery from the land and elevating the people to greater heights of prosperity and security against the day of adversity.

When that day does come, they have a reserve to look to with which they can bridge over the unpropitious season. It is only in agricultural countries that complete immunity can be found from extreme want. The manufacturing interests cannot hold out a certain promise against the day of shortness in the general supply of food. People can wear old clothes, but they cannot eat yesterday's dinner. Agriculture, manufactures, and commerce go well together in times of prosperity, but when adversity comes there is a pot but nothing to boil in it. Hunger cannot admit of the delay incident to trade,—cannot wait for the purchase of food with the wares of the factory; hence the great necessity, which should never be lost sight of by any government, of allowing nothing to retard the agricultural interest,—that being the only secure harbor when the storm is raging without. I would by no means have it understood from the above that the younger members of the family should not be favored and encouraged; but they can only be pensioned off when the accumulations from the entailed estate bring a surplus; economy in the one will bring independence and equality in the other. In pointing out some of the losses besetting the path of agriculture, I do not wish to heap loads on the backs of either of the other two great interests,—manufactures and commerce,—but simply to defend production against carrying the entire burden of the circulating medium of the country,—to protest against its being made to pay all the losses incident to the fluctuations and perils of that medium,—and to insist that the other great interests should be made to contribute in a general average. On this equitable and mutual plan I hope to demonstrate that the circulating medium of an agricultural country, of whatever nature or quality, is peculiarly the property of the producer, and that all the losses, except momentary ones, are finally to be paid by those who made it a necessity, without any hope of participating in the profits, if any. It is as if A, for the honor of being in a firm, should agree to pay all the losses of the bad years, and let B and C divide the profits of the good ones.

Commerce, with its head-light, looks far out to sea, and when going into port she can, if necessary, take on board a pilot. Her facilities are such, from her position and intercourse with nations, that she has invented a peculiar alphabet, by which she can interpret the wants of others and supply her own. Her circulating medium, bills of exchange, checks, credit, etc. are manufactured to suit her convenience. If the trader gets possession of a portion of the circulating medium of a country, he only receives it at its comparative exchangeable value with the products of that country; he instantly parts with it in payment of former purchases, or invests it in new ones. His chance of loss by depreciation is about equal to that of being struck by lightning. Not so with the confiding producer with no debts to pay; he has no resource, but must pocket the loss, whatever it may be. In this way nine-tenths of the losses incident to a circulating medium are distributed over the agricultural portion of the country; while the banker or dealer in money, in times of fear and peril, invests his reserve in bills of exchange, calling for some other medium predicated upon the produce of the country. In this manner all is worked back on the productive interests of the country—on the gross produce—the manufacturer participating sparingly in the depreciation, from the fact that the trader, like the railroad train, carries a front and back light, warning those nearest to him to look out.

If this position as to the true tendency of the money of account be correct, is it not the duty of the government that has the power to regulate the currency and medium of value to furnish, to those who have the losses to pay, such a standard and legal tender as they can at all times have in sight—one that always carries its own light and fog signals? If the loss or depreciation does come, it will be in such a medium as they have a common interest in, and, though inconvenient at the moment to foot up in bulk, the consolation that they have finally to work it out will be some set-off to the summary process of payment. When it finally goes down and becomes worthless, they can still fall back on first principles,—the products of the field,—without which manufacture and commerce cannot exist for one moment. With it, to an amount sufficient for one year's support of labor, prosperity will again come to the aid of its handmaids and copartners in production.

CIRCULATING MEDIUM AND LEGAL TENDER.

It being conceded that a circulating medium and legal tender is a necessity, in a country which has commodities to exchange, you have but to limit this to the actual requirements of production and consumption to invest it with all the values belonging to the commodities to be exchanged. From this moment it has a new and, it might be said, an intrinsic value coequal with the exchange it can effect, and all nations desiring those particular commodities will associate in their estimates the values not of the medium, but of the goods it will purchase. If a country wills that its productions have no more value than the medium, or that so much will be given in exchange, from that moment the medium or standard becomes of equal value with the commodities it will exchange for. Values measure the medium, and the medium measures values. Necessity, after all, is the governing law, and without a desire this necessity would not be produced. The moment you clothe the medium with a purchasing power, it will have the same value as the goods that will purchase it, and it will be so invested with value by all countries connected with the purchase, sale, and consumption of the commodities that can be had in exchange for it. From this moment it has, and with all the world, the values that are given to the particular commodities of that country.

In addition to the foregoing values credited to a particular medium, when it has performed this office and been invested with the power of a legal tender, all creditors become its friends and advocates, which is calculated still further to enhance the value. When the creditor parted with his goods for the promise of this particular legal tender, he affixed to it the values of the commodities for which it would exchange; and, as the recipient of the medium is not likely to undervalue it, it may be taken for granted that he who is compelled to receive it as a legal tender will not lend himself to its depreciation. All legal tenders and mediums are conventional, and no law can invest them with a greater value than the commodities that can be had in exchange for them.

Bonds and time obligations have not this present value of the medium, but are measured by the future promise of return. The medium of exchange is provision stored up for daily consumption; time obligations are promises of the future, and are valued by the certainty of a return. The value of time obligations is measured by their present worth; if discounted, the rate of discount will be fixed in accordance with the security given and the certainty of return of the legal tender. If this obligation be gold, you instantly turn over in your mind the amount of commodities it will purchase to aid reproduction. Should it happen that this commodity, gold, will not command the necessaries and conveniences for sustaining labor, it loses its value, and its mining must cease. After all, you must go back to the universal standard for a measure of values as well as of legal tender, and that is the sustaining power of human labor, and that labor, again, must be measured by the surplus it can produce over consumption. Now, as all values are comparative, the same process of reasoning will be gone through to get at the value of a circulating medium and legal tender. How much of the surplus of others will it command? How much pork, flour, etc.? If this amount be in quantity equal to what gold will purchase, then the values are the same.

If gold be the legal tender and circulating medium of a country, it may become redundant, and be compelled to seek markets offering greater inducements. When this is the case, the speculations of the home market, and orders of foreigners for their balances, may so narrow down the circulating medium that those who desire a legal tender will be so inconvenienced that they may have to sacrifice their commodities or property. This overstocking the market with circulating medium, followed by its sudden withdrawal, from whatever cause, is one fruitful source of all our troubles and misfortunes. Now, if you add to this a depreciation of the circulating medium of credits that are not legal tenders, you have doubled the distress, from the fact that you have destroyed by failure a percentage of the circulating medium at one time relied on to perform the office of a legal tender, while the balance is seeking speculations in other countries. Can this state of things be desirable? Can anything but periodical bankruptcy and universal distress follow? Let the circulating medium and legal tender of our country be, as we desire our government to be, "one and indivisible:" the greatest good will then have been conferred on the greatest number.

It will be readily seen from the foregoing that a depreciation of the circulating medium is not unlike a failure of all the sources of production. All have been sacrificed at the same time (by the receipt of a worthless medium); but if this medium had been fixed to remain a legal tender in the liquidation of debt, the distress from all causes could only be equal to the failure of one commodity, confined to the unfortunates who were engaged in its production. Is not this state of things preferable to universal stagnation and loss from the worthlessness of a medium that had forced all values from the country during its period of prosperity?

No currency or circulating medium, whether of gold or paper, can be kept uniform or stable when used in common by all countries, if the values of the productions of one country differ from those of the same productions in another country. It is what the medium will buy that gives it value. Then why seek for an intrinsic value in a medium that must in its turn be measured by all other values?

The scales by which standards are tested and produce is weighed have no value in themselves, as compared with the commodities gauged. It is not necessary for them to be made of gold: all that is wanted is accuracy. If I place on one side productions, and you place on the other circulating medium to balance, then, when debt takes the place of produce, I wish to see no vibration. If more of the medium be required, let more of debt be canceled. To illustrate further, suppose the grain crops to fail in a country whose circulating medium and legal tender is gold; those who are in want of bread must have it, at whatever sacrifice. Nothing but gold for the moment will purchase it from a foreign country. No sooner do you begin to send off gold than all credit begins to contract. The people are being deprived of a circulating medium and legal tender at the same time, the absence of either of which must derange all trade; and the pressure is intensified by the universal disposition to hoard up the legal tender for a period of greater profit or for additional security in meeting maturing obligations. All this inconvenience and distress can be bridged over, and production will, sooner or later, unlock the hoards of legal tender and circulating medium; but it is very different if the circulating medium be bank-notes, not legal tender, but convertible into gold on demand. This privilege will not give security from an undue quantity being placed in the market. When the reaction begins, all are sensible of the fact, but it is too late to save all the paraphernalia of trade. The greatest losses and calamities ever inflicted on this country have been from the issue of spurious and worthless paper money, forced for a time, through public opinion, to usurp the place of commodities and a legal tender, and when stripped of this sustaining power, not worth, in the liquidation of debt, the paper it was printed on. It is the desire to put a stop to this evil in the future, by the suppression of all local issues to be called money, that prompts the foregoing investigations, and not, as I have already stated, a wish to put property in any man's possession in any other way than by honest industry and for value received. This can be accomplished only through a well-established currency, and this can be attained only by confining the issue to one source, and that must be the government, the power that has the regulating of the legal tender and standard of value. I can see no other reason for the infatuation for a universal gold medium than the indisposition of nations to learn and their reluctance to change. Slow and sure may be the safest rule of conduct in a general way, but when an artery is to be taken up, let us have skill and dispatch, that the patient may not bleed to death.

PRODUCTION AND CIRCULATING MEDIUM.

ADVOCATING, as I have been, the great producing interest of the country, and claiming for it a fair share of legal protection, I only ask that it be exempted from all complications other than its own, by the establishment of a legal-tender medium independent of the complications growing out of the daily speculations in gold, heretofore the universal standard of value. If it be conceded that production is the source of all prosperity, without which no taxes can be collected, and no credit be permanent, it must be acknowledged that it is the duty of the government to throw no stumbling-blocks in its way.

It is argued by many that if we are to have a circulating legal-tender medium not convertible on demand, the fluctuations will be the same as those attending gold. Suppose this should be the case, who will be the sufferer? Will it be the producer, or the consumer?

If speculation conspires to give to the medium more than its true relative value, the productions of those who are not in debt need not be exchanged, and the market can thus be left entirely to those who are in want of a legal tender to meet their maturing obligations. Those who desire a medium of exchange, and are not in want of legal tenders, can wait until a legitimate demand arises for the exchange of their products.

Let us now suppose the reverse of this state of the markets. When combinations of capital have depressed or, for the moment, destroyed the true relative value of the circulating medium, — when but few are in absolute need of a legal tender, and desire only a medium of exchange on new credit to realize the visions of inordinate gain,—speculation will act as a stimulus to increased production, giving to those in want of a legal tender relief from maturing obligations; operating, in fact, as a sort of bankrupt law, since, by a surrender of assets at the enhanced price, they can pay out to the producer not in *want* of a legal tender, but of the medium of exchange, as he has only to wait for the reaction, and the full relative value of the medium will be realized.

Let it be understood, all this is on the supposition that the issuing power of the legal tender is unchangeable, and that no inflation has occurred to give a different relative value to the medium and the production. The reaction will certainly come when the fever of speculation has run its course and past credits begin to mature. However or whenever the circulating medium, if a legal tender, may lend itself to credit and speculation, production will still go on accumulating and laying up for the day of adversity. The howling of the wolves is but evidence that the sheep are close at hand; the prudent owner will take measures to gather his flock into a place of security.

CIRCULATING MEDIUM A NECESSITY.

I do not think there can be any controversy as to the necessity of a circulating medium and measure of value, or legal tender, for those who have incurred debt and desire to discharge it. The capitalist must be aware that no measure of value can be found which will at all times give him the same amount or bulk of production. Gold will not do it; in one country alone the value of annuities fell from one hundred dollars to twenty-five dollars, owing to the great increase in the production of the standard. All are alike deeply interested in the question of finding the standard or medium least liable to fluctuation, or which, after fluctuation, shall have the power to command the largest amount of human productions that are necessary to command labor.

If this be the true position of productive labor and commerce to the currency and legal tender, it is all-important that this medium should be protected from fluctuations by the government as far as that can be done. The daily fluctuation incident to every medium of exchange should have no weight or influence. A promise by the government of so much gold semi-annually may, at the end of twenty years, command as many days' labor as when first issued; the difference between the present value of gold and its value twenty years hence is only a matter of speculation on the part of the capitalist.

Gold, like all other commodities, is liable to rise or fall in value. The tendency, for more than one hundred years, has been to drop it as a circulating medium in the exchange of products. Now, should fashion, which is as changeable as the wind, also discard it, in famine times, mess-pork or flour may be looked upon as having much more permanent value. The losses resulting from these fluctuations should not be visited upon production, the great builder-up of human existence and repairer of the natural decay of time. However prosperity or adversity may mingle together, in the absence of production the one cannot last, nor can the pangs of the other be mitigated,—it is the alpha and omega with a great controlling interest like this, the foundation of all others, without which there would be no need of a circulating medium. How can the government be content to see inflicted upon it all the ills of a vitiated system of currency for the circulation of its products, whose very existence and earnings depend on the contributions from its surplus, whose mistakes and losses are but a forced levy on its enterprise, and which, when prosperity crowns the effort, divides none of the profits with those who paid the losses in times of adversity?

It is now in the power of the government to consult her own interest, and furnish the producer with a legal tender that will be uniform in all parts of the country, that will circulate without discount, and command the fruits of industry wherever found. All will understand, when reading the quotations of pork, flour, etc. in Chicago or New Orleans, that one and the same value is meant, in comparison with the medium; there is now no hesitancy or scruple in regard to the medium we have: all the producers ask is a continuance. The profits and security will all be on their side; and if repudiation from inability should ever come, which no one conversant with the great prosperity and increasing productions of the country can suspect for a moment, the loss will fall on those who reaped the benefit of the profit.

I can imagine but one influence that can possibly cause the government to adopt principles antagonistic to the interest of its people,—an overweening regard for what Mrs. Grundy will say; this may drive her into some wild scheme and repudiation of what she has already inaugurated. The holders of our bonds, if they will consult their own immediate and future interests, cannot but sanction a policy that will give to them a fixed and secure investment in strict accordance with the original contract. What more can they ask than their principal and interest in gold at the stipulated terms? All the difficulties attending the time of payment, or as to the kind of commodity it may be in, will be removed; it is true it will be deprived of the quality favored by the speculator and gambler in value, but it will possess all the requisites of security that are necessary to bring it into favor with capital; it is to this great interest we should appeal, it is from it we receive real value in exchange for our promises, and by its means we hope to rebuild our wasted fortunes and cause each way-spot to be clothed in verdure.

LEGAL TENDER, BALANCE OF TRADE, COTTON CROP, ETC.

In order to a full and perfect understanding of our subject, it is incumbent on us to go back to the beginning and demonstrate the difference between cause and effect. If there was no credit there would be no need for a legal tender. By the disposition to gain and to use all your surplus in reproduction, you are influenced to lend it to those who have not this surplus. From this springs the law of legal tender, in order to enforce a full liquidation of the credit.

If it is gold we have promised as the legal tender, in order to obtain it we are compelled to submit to the universal and unchangeable law of trade, to wit, offer our goods at such prices to those that have gold as will induce them to part with it. When I speak of offering our goods to a country desiring them more than gold, I wish to be understood as including the trader with that particular country. In fact he is, for the time being, the representative of that particular country, so far as trade is concerned. It is this desire for gold on our part, and the commodity on the spot at the moment of our want, that I am endeavoring to obviate, and thus save to the producer the loss attending the delay of importation, which loss is never measured by real value or utility, but by the inexorable law of present necessity.

There is not one transaction in one thousand of our

internal affairs calling for legal tender in liquidation that has the remotest connection with our foreign exchanges; it is to save to the country the losses incident to the nine hundred and ninety-nine transactions that I am now laboring. The internal commerce of a country adjusts itself to its own wants if allowed free intercourse with the foreign, but if fettered with derangements or complications of the merchant or trader, it so mixes up the one with the other that the original producer is always made the scapegoat, or sufferer. It is independence I ask for, and that foreign commerce shall make good its own promises in its own way, and not hold the circulating medium of the producers in the interior responsible for the losses of the trader. If he is so imprudent as to promise a commodity not in the country, it is no reason why the producers of all other commodities should be forced to promise the same. It is as much to the interest of the party having capital to lend it, as it is to that of the borrower to receive it; both are for a *consideration*. Why, then, legislate for a liquidator in favor of the one and not the other?

All countries and all states have enacted laws to stave off or complicate the collection of debt; in some states no property can be sold for cash, or the legal tender, if two-thirds of the value is not bid. This apprized value is made from the comparison of its incomes with the income of other values, and is certainly a great relief to the unfortunate debtor that promised a legal-tender commodity which at that time was not in the country; if it had been here it would have been the true measure of the value of the property, for values measure income, and income measures values. It is not this unfortunate class that I have been laboring to serve, but rather the more numerous and not less deserving class of enterprising traders or adventurers, whose all is staked on their good name and punctuality in footing up the ever-recurring obligations incident to their transactions, that they may not be forced to resort to the technicalities of the law to free them from the promises of a legal tender that could not be commanded until it had been attracted from some distant point.

The great object and effort of the government is to induce the people to produce commodities of value. Then why not give to them a measure that can at all times be found in the country? If it is not unchangeable, it will have the virtue of being always at hand. If the people will play at a game of hazard, let them know the percentage of loss against them; the prudent will be enabled to calculate how long they can hold out against the banker or dealer of the game, and may withdraw in time to save themselves and their families from irretrievable bankruptcy and ruin.

It is not the production of commodities and the large amount of yield in any one year that bring on the country the monetary disasters which periodically exert such baneful influence; it is the want of the average yield, or the shortness in the supply, that brings stagnation and retards for a time the general progress. Complaints of the scarcity of the medium or legal tender may be made when there is or is not an abundance of productions in the country incident to, and caused by, the maturity of obligations based on others and at different times; difficulties such as this are but temporary in their influence and soon right themselves. But when these recovering obligations and legal tenders have to be adjusted from short productions, generally the entire industrial interest becomes involved, and the country is left in a prostrate condition a longer time, not only with more universal distress to the poor, but with the infliction of a permanent injury on all classes, that can be adjusted only by time and compromises. All this internal commotion has but little to do with our foreign exchanges and the balance, so called, of trade, against the country. The government or legislation of the country cannot alter the balance; it can be liquidated only by the parties and individuals interested. If, as a country, we owe a balance on imports over production and have lost money in the transactions, those who enter into the speculation or give the credits must bear the loss, and adjust their differences as best they may. The internal exchanges and debts of a country should not be forced to do more than sympathize with them in the distress of liquidation. Our importers or traders may be unfortunate and *honest*, and the exporters who gave them credit beyond their means may be classed in the same category of unfortunates, and may deserve the sympathy of their friends and country, but let there be no intervention, except in guarding their rights; further than this the government has nothing to do with the balance of trade. After all, the most reliable reports from the exports and imports are only apparent, and not real,—the real balance is only a matter of concern to individuals, and the adjustment of it is their affair, not that of the country. The balance of trade between one section of our country and some other point of the same is of much more importance than any foreign balance, from the fact that we give and take large credits. The balance due New York, the great clearing-house of the interior, has its influence on millions in the country; while that between New York and other countries does not affect even thousands. It is true, the first influence of short production is felt at this great center, but that influence is only paralyzing to trade; with the interior its influence is much greater and far more serious, resulting in the complete stagnation of reproduction. There are two agencies, one or the other of which is all the time influencing the market of export and import, calculated to destroy the even tenor of trade and otherwise derange the financial affairs of a country. The merchant may have overestimated the market and imported too much, and without sales he will be forced into extensions and compromises; or he may have given more credit than production can return in time; in this case the distress is universal, and destructive alike to trade and reproduction.

Between the importer and exporter, compromises and equitable adjustments can be made and trade go on; but not so between the retail dealer and the consumer: the "pound of flesh" must come, and if the creditor be debarred from taking it at once, he will generally sit down for chickens to hatch or the corn to grow. In extreme cases like this, the only sure relief to the productive energies of the interior is through a universal fixed system of bankruptcy, which will allow industry and enterprise to work out a new fortune; the result of which may be a surplus of capital for industry to work upon, and the country will still live and prosper.

The circulating medium of a country measures the value or price of all commodities in the hands of the debtor portion that desire a legal tender to cancel maturing obligations; its influence on that portion not so circumstanced arises only from sympathy and the fear of lower money prices. The result of these influences is to bring down values, in comparison with the measure or legal tender, to a point below the cost of production, until this medium can be attracted from a distant point or some other country; that is to say, when we offer our productions below the natural value or cost price we can get this legal-tender money.

If the prosperous holders that have immediate need of a legal tender to cancel debts would ship their goods or products without drawing a bill, which, if drawn, would be subject to the same sacrifice as the goods, they would avoid the loss incident to a sale in market where others are competing for a legal tender to make good maturing obligations.

From this view of the subject, and its connection with the production and legal tender, it will be seen that the latter measures only that portion of the former which is offered in exchange, and it is only when timidity or fear induces others to follow up the sacrifice that the whole values of the country become involved in the loss incident to the determination to exchange all products for the legal tender. It is at this point light will begin to break in, from the general disposition of the holders or owners of the medium to part with it in exchange for the productions that are offered by wholesale below cost. Now, is it not clear that if the holder of productions who is free from debt and therefore is not forced to sell, would hold over his values, a larger amount of the medium could soon be realized in exchange? The sum total of all is, that our principal sacrifices are mainly due to the debtor class. It is their effort to procure the legal tender that brings on all this train of disasters, the ramifications of which are so great, and exert such a wonderful influence, at times, as to deter many from renewing their efforts to produce articles in universal demand, giving to the more fortunate few a complete monopoly for years. This influence is precisely the same as that of over-production, which, for a time, will send down prices below cost. When the price for cotton ruled so low, in consequence of large production combined with immense indebtedness, to meet which forced sales had to be made, thousands abandoned the culture and invested all their capital in the production of sugar, which in a few years changed the relative prices to such an extent as to bankrupt the latter and enrich the former. When this change did come, those who had embarked in sugar could not go back into cotton, on account of so large an amount of their capital being in sugar-houses, fixtures, etc. Now, all these purgatives are very well, and answer a useful purpose; but it is not necessary to throw the patient into fits in order to rid him of a fever. Supply and demand will regulate themselves in the natural way, without complications with the struggles of individual debtors for legal tender.

I am well aware that much can be said on all sides of this question. At present, however, I deem it best to make but few digressions, as they would complicate a subject that is sufficiently difficult to pursue when holding on to the main thread. No subject has a greater influence on the complications of political economy than this of debt. From it spring most of the intricacies of the law; human passions are fanned into flame, whilst one party is trying to collect, and the other is endeavoring to pay; governments are made and unmade by its creation or extinguishment. Hence I am compelled to ask the reader to be patient and bear with me to the end.

A paper currency not legal tender may be compared to a windmill, whose sails are spread to every breeze, with no governing power, and are swept away by the first gale; but if the currency be made legal tender and limited to the requirements of trade it becomes not unlike the steam-engine, with its governor ready to open or close the valves and accommodate the engine to the resistance offered. This allows human industry to feed up human productions under a well-regulated system of economy in steam. In order that the boiler may not be blown up, the same governing power can be made to close down the dampers, and avoid all waste of fuel, when there is little or no work to be done; in a word, making the government the great fly-wheel to collect and husband the power in order to overcome the greater resistance.

It is a fraud on industry, and a robbery of production, to authorize a circulating medium in a country that is not at the time, and will not be for all time to come, a legal tender. If by common consent it has been exchanged for values, the producer of those values should not be deprived of the power to cancel his maturing obligations with it; for how can he pay when he has parted with the very production he was expected to create when he incurred the liabilities? When this circulating medium was loaned to him, with the view to aid him in production, the lender knew to what extent it would purchase commodities from which reproduction was anticipated; and if the recipient of the loan parts with this new produce for the same medium, there can be no injustice in his tendering it back, together with the stipulated rate of interest, to the original lender. The lender of the medium will then be in the position in which he originally was, to either lend it out or invest it in commodities. He may be able to command more or less of productions than when he first had possession of this medium. This is a risk incident to all exchanges. The producer who borrowed the medium had the same perils to encounter when he sought a market, in order to obtain the means of repayment. It is nothing more than justice to let the profit or loss fall on each adventurer. No man should be expected or required to insure the values of others without an adequate premium. If men will not insure, they must foot up their own losses. Commodities measure commodities. The value of the circulating medium is fixed by the amount it will command of them, and the same process must be gone through to arrive at the intrinsic value of the legal tender. This being the case, is it not unnatural to separate the two and force the seller of productions into bankruptcy for want of a legal tender, when he has just parted with his only asset for a circulating medium that became worthless in the use?

The rapid increase of production and consumption, and the consequent expanse of commerce, with its thousands of miles of railroad and telegraph, demand greater elasticity in the circulating medium, virtually ignoring the old cumbrous road-wagon, gold, except as a remote measure of value. Whilst all these changes are being made, and an elasticity is being given to the circulating medium in the exchange of commodities, let us not force upon the productive industry of the country a speculative medium that cannot, at the moment of need, be converted into a legal tender. Do not let labor be duped any longer with the specious promises of credit, which in the past have proved worthless in the hour of greatest want, and which will always prove so in future. If you give to production a medium of exchange, let it be value received and a liquidator of debt. If we are to run lightning express, let us be sure the company is able and willing to foot up all losses. Should there be any unwilling to enter into the general disposition to receive as a legal tender the circulating medium of the country, they can readily find borrowers who will stipulate to return the same commodity lent; should it be gold, the holder of provisions can call it into being as readily as any other value. Both may fluctuate when compared with each other; one cannot be dispensed with, the other can. The capitalist or lender has the right to stipulate for a return that will satisfy his wants; but the government has no right to permit the infliction of a general circulating medium on a country, to be exchanged for its productions, and not to be used at the same time to liquidate debt.

A circulating medium that is also a legal tender can never suddenly become worthless, or of much less value than when it was originally put into circulation, provided limitation has been such that the amount cannot be increased. Until the last dollar be liquidated, it will still carry a value, and property will be exchanged for it even should production fail to give a surplus; universal and unmitigated distress cannot follow over-trading and wild speculation. Should production fail, wholly or partially, property or fixed capital will only have to retrace its steps and find its original owners. Liquidation will go on, and the result will be only partial bankruptcy, with capital and labor free to rebuild broken fortune.

"FAVORABLE OR UNFAVORABLE BALANCE OF EXCHANGE"—WHAT IT MEANS.

In a previous article I endeavored to explain the nature and effect of the "balance of trade," showing that it was not a national affair, but an individual balance of debt, to be liquidated by the individual. I now propose to pursue the same subject in connection with the balance of exchange for and against a country, in order that much of the mystery attached to it may be cleared away.

If a dealer or banker in New York can get for his draft on London an amount of gold coin more than sufficient to pay the freight, insurance, and transit, the market is quoted at a premium, and the exchange is said to be against us, or unfavorable; in other words, if four dollars and eighty-six cents in New York will not purchase a bill on London for one pound sterling, or one sovereign, then exchange is against New York. Now, what does all this signify? Simply that there is in London more gold than in New York, or that gold is worth more in New York than in London; the indication is not at all times, as is generally believed, that of an excess of importations over exports, or merchandise, or produce. In order that the reader may follow me in the further investigation of this most intricate subject, he must realize the fact that there are two influences constantly at work, and two distinct trades all the time going on; which, however, run into each other occasionally, just as the circulating medium and legal tender become mixed up at times,—a sharp demand for the one operating disadvantageously on the party desiring the use of the other.

We have dealers in every conceivable commodity as well as in gold: the former are constantly calling for a medium of exchange; the latter, for a liquidative or legal tender. The office of the dealer in gold and exchange is double: he undertakes to furnish the dealer in produce with the purchasing power, and the indebted with a legal tender or liquidative; in each case, of course, with a view to profit.

As there is a clear line of separation between the dealer in produce and merchandise, and the dealer in gold circulating medium and legal tender, we must not confound the operations of the one with the other. With this digression we will come back to the bill in New York or London, worth a premium, and said to be unfavorable and indicative of *something*, generally understood to be debt, or an excess of imports over exports. Now, I contend that it is more frequently an evidence of large production and a desire to export than of poverty or debt. A large amount of commodities pressing on the market of New York for export to London, in the shape of bills of exchange, offering to all the banks and dealers for a medium of interior exchange, they must, of necessity, be short of it at times, especially if there are not as many buyers of their bills drawn against the proceeds of this exchange. This shortness of the medium may be, and generally is, such as to cause them to import gold or the legal tender, which tends to force down the price of produce through the discount on the exchange, until the equilibrium has been restored. It is simply an excess of commodities over gold, and, so far from being indicative either of debt or poverty, evinces great prosperity and a large yield of productions, pressing for export in advance of imports. This is one view of the subject. A desire to import in advance of available commodities indicates precisely the reverse, and, in the case of a deficient harvest, causes the excessive exportation of gold, or of the legal tender of the country whose productions are desired, leading those who are in debt, as well as those who desire to speculate, to hold on to as much legal tender as they can command, knowing that it will soon be the most valuable commodity in the country, from the fact that it is in demand for export. The long and short of all this is, the party desiring *food*, or something he fancied he might stand in need of, paid for it with gold, leaving the debtor portion of the community without the means of liquidation, rendering necessary on their part, it may be, even greater sacrifices in the exchange of their products or assets for it, than were made by the party in want of food. In the one case the deprivation is of a luxury—a circulating medium; in the other, of a necessity—a legal tender.

The foregoing will serve to pave the way to a proper appreciation of the concluding portion of this subject, more particularly in its bearing on the general commerce of the country, and on parties interested in this demand for legal tender or gold. We have seen that a medium for the exchange of products is a luxury, and that a liquidator of debt is a necessity: one party is the speculator or creditor, the other the producer. Which of the two deserves encouragement or sympathy? To illustrate, allow me to cite the case of the Bank of England, with her millions borrowed from the country. It is true she has lent to her merchants and traders largely—but not greatly in excess of what they have lent to her in the shape of deposits. Her circulating notes have been given to the country in exchange for its products, and it is to be presumed that a valuable consideration was given at all times. The produce was lent and the notes were borrowed. Let us now suppose that a deficient harvest makes it necessary for the producer to call on the bank for gold, so as to have a legal tender, with which to command food from those who are at the moment supplied with all other commodities. The moment this demand springs up there is great commotion in the debtor class, including the bank, she too being called on for a legal tender in exchange for her notes; the rate of interest is advanced, the export of gold is discouraged, and the cry of "exchange is unfavorable" is raised—all of which means that she is being called on to pay her debts. Suppose she does pay them, as any honest merchant would do, will the country be any worse off, or have fewer commodities to sell or exchange for gold? I can see no reason whatever for special legislation to give her authority not to pay her debts. If capital or credit be allowed to sink the producer, both will find a watery grave; the former must bridge over the stream, in order that productions may safely arrive at a market. If the bank is allowed to issue a medium of exchange for the legal tender, or, in other words, to borrow it, she should pay her debt, when it is demanded, with a good grace; if unable to redeem it in full, she should do as thousands of individuals have been compelled to do,—give up her assets in liquidation, and not try, by a parade of the eternal "balance of exchange," to induce others to think her debt is any more than that of an individual. After having given up all her legal tender and property, still having notes in existence, it may be an inconvenience to the country to lose the amount, but she will still have all the values and products she had before.

The moral is, no notes should be allowed as a circulating medium that are not a legal tender. The loss will then be equitably divided among those who have them to pay and those who receive them. One fruitful source of loss and ruin will be removed. Speculators may inflate prices, and finally fail from a want of ability to make good the deficiencies between the buying and the selling price; it will be for them to fight it out. The producer will have something left in exchange for his assets by which he can cancel debt. The law calls for a valuable consideration to make a binding contract. Give it to production, and you will have conferred on it a priceless boon. The incubus of doubt and uncertainty will be lifted from industry, and honest labor will be defended from fraud and the allurements of the gambling speculations of those who endeavor to live by their wits alone. The storm may howl without and fill every harbor with the wrecks of commerce, but the interests of production are secure: they are under their country's protection, and in this hour of need can lend a helping hand to man the "life-boat," in order to succor perishing friends.

LEGAL-TENDER CIRCULATING NOTES NOT MADE LEGAL TENDER, A CURSE TO PRODUCTION.

A THOROUGH investigation of the entire subject in relation to its bearings on commerce and individual interests involved—the necessity of a circulating medium to effect the exchanges of the country—forces me to a conclusion considerably at variance with the majority of those most deeply interested in its details, especially in regard to the benefits claimed to arise from a circulating medium and legal tender. All will admit the impossibility of effecting the exchanges of a country without a circulating medium. It is my purpose now to show who should be the recipient of the profits or tax on production. I take it for granted that no one will differ with me as to the distribution of the gain from the use of the medium, or as to who should bear the loss incident to the maintenance of a circulating medium, when I show the value of the services rendered to commerce and the real benefit conferred upon trade.

At the outset I take the position that a circulating medium for the exchange of productions is a curse to a country if that country does not make it a legal tender; it inflicts on its industry all the losses incident to its use, leaving the interior trade of the country, in times of doubt and peril, without compass or rudder, to say nothing of the wild ventures placed on unseaworthy crafts fitted out by reckless speculators. To shield the unsuspecting from losses in no wise connected with their business or interest, I now labor to draw the line between capital and credit: the one is sure to build up a country; the other may dissipate its wealth by imprudent risks.

I am in favor of all due encouragement to both, but desire to see them in the hands of industry and prudence: hence my opposition to banks of circulation, which issue notes that cannot be made legal tender at the moment of necessity, when they have absorbed the productions of industry. The most serious objection to this position, and, in fact, the only one of any importance, is, how can we produce discounts and loans to prosecute works of enterprise in the absence of capital?

Allow me to answer by asking a few questions: When you borrow the notes of a bank, the best that can be devised,—say the Bank of England,—what do you get for your notes and the promised rate of interest for time? Notes payable on demand, or convertible into the gold or products of the country; otherwise they would be worthless to you.

After you have the notes they are not capital, nor

the means of reproduction; nor are they the food of industry or labor. After you have converted them into commodities to aid production, you have added nothing to what was already in existence in the country. In this case you have borrowed no *capital*, but a credit. If you attempt to draw gold to export in exchange for something to aid industry, the loan will be refused, or usurious rates of interest will be demanded.

This is virtually a prohibition to production. You are generally forced to retire these credits when the bank finds she is not being credited as usual. After all, you have only borrowed a credit or purchasing power for the time being, for which you have paid interest, and, whatever depreciation may occur, the individual holders must lose, as it is not a legal tender. If this is all, why may not the government furnish this circulating medium to the country, saving it the tax for interest, and let its people know when they part with their productions that they have instituted a legal tender with which they can, without further sacrifice or loss, discharge their debts? When you wipe out all circulating notes from the medium of exchange, other than the legal tenders of the government, you have left in the country the same materials to support labor as you would have if there were a bank at every cross-road. Let us have banks, but let them be banks of discount for collecting together the scattered and idle capital of the country, and lending it to its people.

Prudence will characterize their loan of capital; while ruin and inflation will grow out of the loan of credit, or circulating notes,—which is the same thing, in a more objectionable form, as the losses fall most heavily on the poor in times of disaster and trouble.

If the means of putting labor in motion be still in the country, it will be husbanded and concentrated in these banks of discount when exchanged for legal tenders. Then the greatest amount of loans can be made that prudence and reproduction will require, all of which will be based on real capital; otherwise, the loan of credit may engulf both lender and borrower.

I do not claim the same benefit to production from an extended system of credits that many do,—real value. Such commodities as are the loss and return of the producer receive no more credit than usage has fixed,—to wit, a sixty days' sight bill, which follows the produce, no loser intervening, and foots itself up independent of a legal tender, as its conversion, after all, is into other commodities.

The credits are sought and obtained to bring the goods and wares of the merchant and trader to the door of the consumer.

The temptation, in nine cases out of ten, for the sake of gain on the one part, and from the desire to consume on the other, is such that the flattering but delusive prospects of the future will bring distress and ruin to both.

There is no country possessing the necessaries and conveniences of reproduction that will not lend them to its industrious and economical people. Prosperous production rarely fails to find capital and friends. It may be said that prosperous production sustains and gives all credit that has a favorable end. Then why force it on the unsuspecting consumer, when it may bring ruin to himself and his principal?

Credit will inflate, but capital will build up and bridge over its mistakes, if in the hands of industry, economy, and enterprise.

Banks of circulation lend *credit*, but often borrow capital to a much larger extent, and rarely use it in a lasting or profitable manner,—in reproduction in the country. How can the dealers in credit know the food of production? Inflation and chance are the only words in their vocabulary. Their allurements may have enabled speculation to send to the remotest ends of commerce the only true liquidator of debt in exchange for their worthless promises. This may have been gold or mess-pork, it matters not which to the producer. The legal tender has been lost to him, and he is now required to sacrifice his reserve, in order honorably to discharge an obligation. A failure to do this may completely stagnate future energy, so as to complicate fraternal feeling with vulgar lucre, or to allow dissipation and indolence to usurp the place of honest toil.

DEBT, INTEREST, AND LEGAL TENDER.

In summing up all the arguments in defense of the position I have taken for the divorcement of the legal tender of the country from gold or any other article of merchandise, and, finally, through the saving to the country of the annual interest or profits from a capital so large as its circulating medium, by the substitution of legal tender based on the public debt, I come to the consideration of the influence of those who may happen to own or be the recipients of the annual interest on this debt. And, as the position I am about to take is somewhat at variance with that of the majority of those who profess to have opinions on political economy, and of those who take their thoughts at second-hand, it is necessary for me to go back to the foundation of the debt and the causes of its creation, in order that the whole subject may come up in review for consideration on its merits.

However men may differ as to the policy which led to the creation of our indebtedness, none can deny that it is an established *fact*, amounting to at least $2,500,000,000, and that it is our duty as a nation to see that it be honorably paid. An ordinary debt, contracted to meet a deficiency of annual receipts, calls for an effort on the part of the government to pay it promptly; but where the sum has been lent for the purpose of maintaining the national existence, patriotism—the highest incentive to moral action—compels us to renewed exertion, in order that final restitution may be made and no loss accrue to those who came forward to our relief in time of doubt and peril.

It being admitted that we owe the money, it must likewise be admitted that we cannot at present pay it, but must give a consideration to those who will lend us the means to discharge the same; and here begins my divergence from the usually received ideas as to whom it should be owing to, or who should be the recipients of the annual interest.

The capital of this debt has been sunk forever, so far as this government is concerned; and other capital must be called into being from which the principal and annual interest are to be paid, provided we are not able to advance it. If we were able to do without this large sum in production, there could be no further argument as to the course proper to be pursued; honor and prudence would say, Pay the debt at once; but, as we are not able to do so, we must endeavor to find who will let us have the means of liquidation for the smallest rate of interest or annuity.

The security for repayment which the government can offer to its creditors, it must be conceded, will enable it to negotiate its loans at much lower rates of interest than would be granted to private individuals. It is true there are a few capitalists in the country who could negotiate a loan on as favorable terms as the government. They will be the first to come forward and invest their savings at the market rate of such credits. Now, the question narrows itself down to this: If the abstraction of so large a sum from the enterprise of the country should have an unfavorable or destructive effect on its productive power, and if we can realize a larger profit from the use of this sum in the development of resources, and finally lessen the burden in the liquidation of our own debt by the creation of other and larger means to abstract it from, it certainly will be to our interest to insist on the government's borrowing; if she can command capital at four per cent. per annum, it is better than for individuals to take the same from production and have to borrow at eight per cent. to fill the vacuum. Hence it is to our interest to negotiate with those who offer the best terms. In this we must know no country, but look only to the rate per annum, and adopt the lowest. If this loan should be offered by our own people, it will be evidence of past economy, and will redound to the credit of our country. If other countries offer better terms than our own citizens can afford to take the loan at, it will be evidence that they too have been economical, but are without channels of income still open to us, and yielding larger profits; hence the inducement they will have to invest in our securities; it is capital cheaper than any we have to offer; it is simply borrowing at four per cent. and using the capital at eight per cent. We cannot but profit by the difference. If I can get the use of one hundred bushels of corn for a promised increase of four, and it should, when used in production, yield me one hundred and twenty, I will have left sixteen to be used in consumption or production; while the lender gets four bushels for my use of the hundred, I will be the gainer of sixteen. It is this very influence that prompts us to trade with any country. Can we better our condition? There is no difference between profits in interest and profits on productions. The question is, simply, Will the intercourse better my condition? It matters little to me who gets the four bushels of corn, since I have sixteen left for my own use. There can be no controversy as to the effect of the public debt being owned by its citizens, and letting the interest abstract nothing from the country. It is like taking money out of one pocket and putting it into the other. Now, I contend that it is equally true that it would be more profitable to take ten dollars out of one pocket and put eleven dollars in the other.

An effort has been made to induce Congress to place on the market a loan of $1,200,000,000 at an interest of not over four and a half per cent. per annum. This will save to the country thirty-three and one-third per cent. of the annual charge. If the loan be taken at four per cent., the saving and reduction will be fifty per cent. Now, would it not be the course of wisdom to call in a competitor who will, if allowed, take one-half the sum free of charge, and make the loan perpetual, instead of for twenty years, or, what amounts to the same thing, pay off the debt and rid the country of its ever-recurring semi-annual tax? This competitor is found in the citizens of the country, who, as they have both debt and interest to pay, should certainly be consulted. They not only offer to take up now one-half of this loan, or $600,000,000, but will engage to cancel in the same way, annually, no less a sum than $50,000,000. They contend that this formidable competition, at the time the loan is being negotiated, will be such an evidence of good faith that the balance will be taken up at lower rates of interest; and that if they maintain their promise for a few years in the prompt payment of interest and the annual reduction of the debt by $50,000,000, the rate will fall, in about fifteen years, to three per cent., especially by the maturity of the ten-forty bonds.

If the people of a great producing country like this say they are satisfied to exchange their annual productions for a legal-tender circulating medium, which the government has the power to furnish them, what better security can be offered than such values as the world cannot dispense with? Can a country give stronger evidence of good faith than a permanent and continuous investment to so large an amount? No constitution or law can be half so binding; either may be repealed or become susceptible of misconstruction, but when a people invests in a security that promises only an annual benefit or convenience, in the language of Sydney Smith when speaking of Pennsylvania bonds, "it is a permanent investment; there can be no withdrawal." The effect on the finances of the country of giving to the people what they demand, to wit, a uniform measure of value and circulating medium, one that cannot consume productions by supporting idle adventurers, and which cannot be influenced by fluctuations resulting from speculation inside and outside of the "ring,"—since the same amount of values will be in the country,—cannot be other than beneficial. No one can deny that there will be a saving to the people of six per cent. per annum on $600,000,000, or $36,000,000. Not only so: the amount is double, as I can demonstrate without resorting to Dr. Franklin's "Penny Saved." If the circulating medium of a country is as necessary to its commerce as to production, it is worth precisely the same rate of interest per annum whether used in the one or the other. This being the case, $600,000,000 at six per cent. will cost $36,000,000. Now, suppose that by the use of my own paper in the same channel I save the payment of the $36,000,000, the total amount would be $72,000,000. To make this a little clearer, let us suppose England should offer to lend the United States $600,000,000 for the sum of $36,000,000, and then, to accommodate us further, should lend us a like sum of Bank of England notes, to be used as a circulating medium, for a like annuity of $36,000,000, would she not annually abstract from us $72,000,000? If we could do no better, this would be a very favorable offer, and we should by all means accept it, rather than resort to the most favored banking institution ever established in this country. None of them ever lent us their circulating notes long at a time for less than double this rate of interest, as is proved by the amount of their annual dividends over all the losses and expenses incident to trade. If to this $72,000,000 be added the annual promised reduction of $50,000,000, and the consequent saving in interest, and its rate at compound interest for a few years be calculated, the vast benefit to production resulting from the economy and security of a uniform medium will become apparent. Manufactures and commerce cannot languish long under increasing productions, but will in their turn stimulate new and grander efforts.

MEDIUM OF EXCHANGE.

The circulating medium should have no other value than as a medium. By limiting it to the demand, it will remain uniform and will have no disturbing influence on commodities, as is the case if it has intrinsic value.

Exports buy and pay for imports, whether of goods or gold. Imports banish gold from the country.

When gold was the legal tender and medium of exchange, the exports had to purchase it at an expense of five per cent. per annum on an average, through the discount on bills drawn against export articles or produce. All this was needed to keep up the supply required as a medium and legal tender in the interior of the country. All shipments had to pay this charge, when but a small portion, if any, was needed by the producer as a legal tender. Even the banks exacted this, in order to be protected against the results of an imprudent issue of their notes; when the market became panicky, they doubled the charges, so that if the gold did not return in time through the accustomed channels, it might be forced through express messengers.

Exports paid annually $25,000,000 to keep up the supply of gold medium. This sum was largely used by importers as a discrimination against domestic manufactures,—the cheap exchange enabling them to bring in goods at a profit that otherwise could not have been imported. The exchange is as much an item in the cost as freight or any other charge. The price reacts with the reaction in exchange, precisely as it does now with gold. This large sum is a dead loss to the producer, and is nothing more than a bounty to the foreign manufacturer.

To keep up a medium costs the country the average rate of interest for money on both securities. If we use $600,000,000, the cost at six per cent. is $36,000,000. Who should be the recipients of this sum? It certainly should be the people who adopt it as a medium and make it a legal tender.

Lessening the demand or increasing the supply of commodities tends to cheapen them in price. If we discard gold as a medium, we lessen the demand to some extent, and consequently cheapen it. This influence will be felt by all countries holding gold. More of it will be given for our exports. This being one of the laws of trade, the converse holds good. With our substituted legal tenders, internal exchange will go on with increased regularity, and the export or import of gold will have no more influence than the sending off of so much cotton and the return of wines and silks. We produce to consume. It is the amount of production that enables us to buy or sell.

Government credit is measured solely by the surplus of production over consumption. No country ever surrendered its stock in trade in payment of debt: to do so would be a change of nationality; hence the debt is a bond on income over consumption.

Bills of exchange, as now used, are the purchasing power and medium between exports and imports, especially between the raw produce of the country and a great part of the imports. In the absence of undue fluctuations, value commands the legal tender on which the bills are drawn, and *their* legal tender commands the commodities we desire to import. From a mutual exchange both countries derive their profit to the extent of the gratification of these desires. The medium of exchange adds no value to the commodities, nor does it give a country new products. Its office is to find the surplus of one party to be used by the other.

Abundance depresses prices, and scarcity elevates them. Values are in the inverse ratios. One is wealth, the other is poverty; one is sleek and fat, the other is lean and gaunt.

On the next page I place a diagram to illustrate and simplify the position I have taken in regard to the comparison of values based upon a medium having no intrinsic value beyond the commodities it will exchange for or command. With this scale and a price-current before you, the relative exchange value can easily be found. Suppose the scale to represent the supply at the prices affixed in accordance with a legitimate demand, and with the prin-

Outfit for Labor	1000	Thousands.
1 bale Cotton	100	Hundreds.
Outfit of Clothing	50	
	40	
	30	
1 bbl. Pork	20	Double Eagle.
100 lbs. Sugar	10	Tens. Eagle.
	9	
50 lbs. Coffee	8	
	7	
	6	
1 bbl. Flour	5	½ Eagle.
$100 at Interest	4	
	3	
1 bbl. Potatoes	2	
100 lbs. Salt	1	Units. Dollar.
	0	

ciple of giving to labor and capital the same return from the production of the one article as the other, in the open market one bale of cotton will exchange for—

An Outfit of Clothing	50
1 bbl. Pork	20
2 " Flour	10
100 lbs. Sugar	10
50 lbs. Coffee	8
1 bbl. Potatoes	2
	$100

If the medium can be exchanged for all the above commodities, it will buy the bale of cotton. Then the grower of four bales of cotton will be able with one to clothe and feed the laborer; with another he can pay rent, or ten per cent. on $1000, and with the remainder he can support and educate a family of five; or, in other words, the laborer that can save up this $1000 can accomplish all this when too infirm to work.

Endless combinations and compromises can be made. If one barrel of pork sells for $20 in gold, then five barrels of pork will command one bond of $100, or one bale of cotton, or twenty barrels of flour. Again, suppose a failure of production in any one article of prime necessity; the decrease of the supply will enhance the prices of the scale. The owner of the bale of cotton will now be forced to dispense with some of the luxuries, and so on with all producers to mankind. This is a positive loss. Human labor does not receive or enjoy its accustomed reward.

Now, take the most favorable view of human labor and its returns from a greater intimacy with capital.

Let all products be doubled, wealth will be doubled, human enjoyments will be in the same ratio, and the relative value of products will remain the same. If the volume of the medium remains unchanged, its value will be enhanced. If it be also doubled, relative prices will be the same, interest remaining the same; but if it be not doubled in the same proportion, interest will be doubled, as there will be a greater demand for capital in the building up of new labor to gratify human wants and desires. As you increase quantities you decrease prices. Population remaining the same, you increase wealth or the power to enjoy the necessaries, conveniences, and luxuries of life. The general lessening of prices increases the abundance of enjoyments. With increased production new wants spring up. This is the great stimulus to incessant production, and from which all communal prosperity springs. If these new desires cannot be gratified at home, foreign trade supplies them with the conveniences and luxuries of other countries. Here a local legal-tender medium displays its greatest powers in the distribution and economy of the surplus fruits of human labor, and demands no sacrifice in the hunting up of a medium further than a change in the rates of interest sufficient to induce the holder of four per cent. bonds to convert them into a medium equal to the increased products of the country, thus giving back to the fortunate laborer nearly a full return of other men's surplus in exchange for his excess.

The commodity whose supply is increased should not have its exchangeable value destroyed by being forced to hunt up a legal-tender medium that has no elasticity; it should only contribute to the payment of the enhanced price of the goods desired in return, resulting from the new or increased demand. This in many instances cannot be great, from the fact that nearly all men hold a surplus of some one thing which they would be willing to exchange for the increased production. This will give an opportunity to effect the exchange not before offered. Whatever the increase in the value of other commodities, it will be equally distributed; no one will be the loser, and the fortunate holder of the increased product will have the chance to enjoy the full benefit of his good fortune.

If foreign luxuries are desired, there must be a surplus of home products to give in exchange for them. If there are cheap facilities for export, and no unnecessary restrictions imposed by the importation of a legal-tender medium, we may hope for an equitable exchange of surplus commodities; it is absolutely necessary that there be a clear understanding of the relative position of products, one to the other, before any change of policy can be hoped for.

There may be in Europe a glut of many articles much desired by the growers of grain in America, of which we may have a glut. The one will relieve the other, and do all that human labor can accomplish, in adding to the enjoyments of life, or contributing to reproduction. Commodities may be ill distributed, but there can be no *general* glut.

Industry under ordinarily favorable circumstances

will produce a surplus of commodities. It should then be the effort of capital and commerce to cheapen charges and facilitate transportation; then a larger amount of goods can be brought back in return, with increased power to consumers,—since the producer would rather pay ten per cent. on his profits than the regular commissions of two and a half per cent. on gross sales. The power of the consumer to purchase enables the merchant to sell and accumulate.

A more than average increase of productions resulting from a favorable season—there being a legitimate desire for them, and a surplus to buy them with—should not lower the exchangeable value of the increased products; it may raise the value of those to be exchanged for them.

There is a point around which exchangeable values vibrate. This is found by the worth of capital and sum of human labor in the production. A permanent deviation from this point will attract or repel the efforts to produce; and this is self-regulating, and should not be interfered with by any artificial regulations in effecting the exchanges. To make the position more apparent, underwriters make good the losses of bad seasons from the accumulations of the good; to lower the rate of premium in prosperity would bankrupt them in adversity. A profitable scale of mortality in the expectancy and insurance of life will not do to use in the granting of annuities.

There is an oft-repeated saying that half a crop will fetch as much money as a whole one. This will be the case where the medium has no elasticity and cannot expand with the production, compelling the laborer to lose its enjoyments in the same ratio, depriving him of the abundance which nature gave him and intended he should enjoy. If a man happens on a streak of good luck, allow him to treasure it up to aid him when the day of misfortune comes.

I am well aware that the cost of productions is measured by labor, below which point it cannot remain for any length of time; nor can it rise permanently above it. It is the profits from the accidental streak of good luck that I wish to economize for use when a reverse shall come. If life and human exertion were one constant even flow of power to enjoy and consume, there would be no need of a great fly-wheel to accumulate force, in order to overcome the terrible resistance of adversity, which the ordinary momentum may not be able to accomplish. Let us lay up a reserve from times of prosperity, in order that, when the great tilt-hammer has to be raised, no perceptible diminution of motion can be seen in the machinery. Let us no longer run this great machine of production and consumption without a fly-wheel. Do not force us to compare all products by one; if so, you will at one time have to conform to the standard or measure. If you make one bushel of wheat, it is called a bushel; if two, let it not be called one; if a half bushel, it is only a half bushel. Let us have a rule that will work both ways. If one bushel of wheat be the equivalent of ten yards of calico, then I claim twenty yards for two bushels, and will not complain at receiving five yards for half a bushel. I am willing that my misfortunes shall abridge my enjoyments; but when the good fortune comes, let me have the full benefit of it; do not force me to make a voyage around the Horn when I can make the journey by rail and save time and expense. When I offer my increased product, and you have nothing from the average to exchange for my surplus, do not undervalue mine by comparing it with gold, but allow me to make the best exchange I can, though I may have to go to a foreign country to effect it.

Values buy and exchange for values, whatever the medium may be. If of intrinsic value, its original cost, together with its added value as a legal tender, must be estimated; if conventional, it will be measured by the commodities for which it will exchange, leaving all commodities free to exchange for each other. Then, if I have pork and desire flour, I will not have to ask the price of gold or cotton in effecting an equitable exchange. No extraneous elements will have to be called in to disturb the harmony of our values. If I want gold at any time, I will measure my values by the cost or value of gold, and will not be forced to pay the extra price consequent upon its having been made by law a legal tender. If I do not like the terms offered in exchange, I will consult my next greatest need, which may be a milch-cow. If as plenty as pork, there will be no difficulty in effecting an exchange; if not, the option will be left to call on cotton to import me the gold. This is the simple history and great truth, and forces the conclusion that the medium should have no intrinsic value, and should be at all times a legal tender, like our greenbacks, and, to give it elasticity, should be made interchangeable with four and a half per cent. bonds: then the rise or fall of the medium will conform to large or small productions, freeing us from the financial complications of other countries. If the producer part with his goods for a medium not legal tender, and then be informed by his creditor that the bank or insurer has exploded, how can he pay his debts, having parted with his assets?

A medium and legal tender interchangeable with four per cent. bonds will have the ultimate value of a four per cent. annuity. When no greater value presents itself in exchange, it cannot remain long below this point; while it is being exchanged for other values and used as a medium, the government will be benefited to the amount of the interest saved.

Secure to *industry* and *economy* their honest dues, and increased productions will be the result. There can be no greater incentive held out to labor than uninterrupted possession in all the transformations and exchanges of its products. Nothing tends sooner to dampen the ardor of man than insecurity; his disasters are not confined to himself,—the blighting effects are soon felt by trade and commerce.

The large demand on this country for cotton by England tends to cramp their market for discounts, from the fear that the amount may not be covered by their exports, causing a heavy demand on the banks for gold, or unfavorable balance of exchange. This is especially the case when the bills against this cotton begin to mature, causing speculators and spinners to ask for large discounts to aid them in carrying stock, resulting often in the prostration of the market, and reacting on the balance of our crop of cotton to go forward. Now, if we had no calls for gold as a legal-tender medium, their fears would be dissipated to a considerable extent, and our exports would be paid for, as usual, by our imports of their surplus, each party realizing a steady market, and, at least, exemption from the ruinous disasters incident to so large a trade,—more especially when European complications tend to war, forcing capital to the great centers for protection against any unfavorable balance of trade.

EXCHANGE AND MEDIUM.

I feel confident that no one well acquainted with the course of the exchange market will contend that the business of a large crop of any or all exportable commodities can be effected so cheaply, and with so little friction or derangement to trade and liquidation of debt, as it is now done with our inconvertible legal-tender medium. If you will look fairly and squarely at the object and purpose of a medium on productions, which is but consumption and reproduction, you will find that the effort of all those who have a surplus is to exchange it for the largest amount of other people's goods. When this is the case, a greater impetus is given to productions; and without being thus stimulated, consumption cannot go on to the extent that will bring the greatest benefit to the largest number.

If it be, as I have stated, a positive benefit to productions to make use of a local legal-tender medium in the sale and exchange of man's surplus, then it is a curse to inflict on them a medium without elasticity, that cannot be used freely without exerting a disturbing influence in the buying and selling exchange, the discount on which must be a loss to the producer, as well as to the trader, who can import with safety only to the extent of the exports, and consequently must lose the profits on the increased trade now thrown away.

These losses are greatest in times of prosperity, when large exports are pressing on the market, and dealers in exchange are compelled to advance the rate of discount to cover the delay and expense incident to getting returns per express, or when imports are coming in freely, requiring the exchange to pay for them. Many large importers, whose capital is larger than their ordinary business will absorb, avail themselves of these favorable opportunities to cover not only their past imports, but to provide in advance for new ones, frequently realizing larger profits by the discount than the ordinary charge for importing. Still, after all, the losses fall entirely on the producer of the exports.

I cannot adduce better proof of the correctness of this position than the workings of our present exchanges for the past few years, under the influence of the legal-tender act; the variations at no time having exceeded the charges necessary to cover bills by shipment of coin. Now I contend that a further saving on this will be effected so soon as a four per cent. bond can be converted into legal-tender medium, from the fact that all large dealers in foreign bills will keep by them, as a *reserve*, bonds to fall back on, in case currency should grow scarce from a large pressure of bills on the market against the producer of the interior for export. This position of the market is sure to occur annually at the South, on account of her large export of cotton, a small amount of which produces a large sum of exchange. The discount of one-half to one per cent. on a bond bill will tempt the holder of the four per cent. bond to convert it into the medium, in order to realize this extra interest.

The great incentive to deal in exchange is the rapid movement in buying and selling the capital. Being turned over many times, even at one-eighth to one-quarter per cent., it realizes in the aggregate a large interest per annum; a running liability of $10,000,000 will give for the year over $100,000,000 of business and a profit of over $100,000 from a capital of not more than $500,000, which must be kept well in hand, with no dead weight or extra-hazardous risks. In insurance it is the small premiums for good risks that pay best.

The above profits will also inure to the benefit of the interior dealer in checks and bills; he too will keep his reserve in bonds, in order to command the medium on the spot, so as not to be forced to send off his bills for discount, to be sent back in currency, with express charges and loss of interest.

Take the position of the buyer of a sterling bill against cotton. Suppose, before the consignment arrives in Europe, a large demand resulting from war complications is made on the Bank of England for coin; immediately up goes the rate of interest and down goes cotton, as it must be sold to pay the bill. This decline may be so great that the bill will be dishonored and fall back on the dealer or banker. It is these sharp turns in the market that bring on the trade nearly all the losses, sweeping from the stage both the drawer and the buyer of the exchange. At this point panics generally set in, and react on the producer, not only lowering the price of what he may have for sale, but involving him in ruin, if the medium he receives for his cotton proves not to be a legal tender, which is likely to be the case if it be bank-notes.

You may answer that if the medium be national bank-notes the government will take care of them. She may at that very time, however, be in such a position that it will be impossible for her to do so.

If we divorce ourselves from gold at once, few sharp angles will have to be turned. With this disturbing element out of the way, all parties will be better able to calculate the chances, as they will be conformed generally to the estimate of stocks in the different markets and the probable demand. Statistics and price-currents will give very accurately this information as to supply and stock.

In regard to gold, we have been without reliable

data, and must continue so, from the fact that its course is so erratic. A speck of war, no bigger than a man's hand, may upset the best-laid plans of men and governments. No one can foresee when the timid will begin to hoard gold, nor how long they will withhold it from the channels of trade. It is not so with cotton or food. Hunger will force sales of the latter, and general as well as individual interest will force consumption of the former, in order to buy the food and keep the millions from idleness and want.

TRUE BASIS OF ALL MEDIUMS.

WHATEVER the medium may be, it neither adds to nor diminishes the quantity of commodities on sale. Then why should it be an exportable article, with the power, when short in supply, of disturbing the relative exchangeable values of all other productions?

The interior banking companies frequently run short of currency and lose the opportunity to take all the bills against produce seeking export points, and are compelled to forward these bills to the great commercial centers for discount, and to have currency sent back to them by express in return. If the conversion of four per cent. bonds into the medium were admissible, a large portion of this expense would be saved to the stockholders and immediate neighborhood, causing them to invest a large portion of their capital in these bonds, in order to be prepared to buy all the bills against the crop, knowing that the season's imports will consume the exchange, and realizing two profits instead of one.

The circuit of the medium must be made. The producer pays it to the retail dealer for goods and for debt, he to the banker for bills on the country from which he desires to import goods, and the banker passes it back to the buyer of the country produce against his bill. Prosperous productions throughout the country call for an increased supply of the medium. When this extra demand no longer exists, that portion of the medium at last will seek a four per cent. bond, from the fact that it can be sent for at any moment to engage in hunting up surplus commodities for sale.

Civilization and the multiplication of commodities create new desires, that cannot be gratified by the productions of one man's labor; hence the necessity of exchange for the surplus of others, in order that the wants of each may be supplied; and this necessity gives rise to the employment of a medium.

If you take into consideration the importance of a medium, and then weigh the use and find out the object, you will be better able to judge of the kind that is needed, and will know the greatest number of wants.

In the first place, you are compelled to have a medium in order that commodities may be exchanged in the supply of man's innumerable wants.

As many supply these wants by purchases of goods on time, they can only safely sell when they are getting in exchange something that will liquidate debt. This is why I have made the point that all mediums should be a legal tender; if the process of liquidation be not all the time going on, sales of commodities will to a large extent cease to be made; certainly credits will cease to be given. I know of no greater stimulus to exertion than the desire to sustain credit. The wish to acquire property is not greater than the wish to liquidate debt promptly; many traders have little other capital than honor and promptness, and hence their extraordinary exertions to compass the means of payment. These parties buy on time and sell for the difference over cost.

This position of the seller of commodities for a liquidator will be rendered more apparent by taking into consideration the double office of the medium, —the exchange of produce, and the liquidation of debt.

The gross produce of the country is over $3,000,000, and the running debt nearly $8,000,000; at least one-third of the gross products are consumed at home by the producer, and for this, of course, no medium or liquidator is required; then the $2,000,000 must be exchanged for other goods: if for cash, the medium must be used; if on time, and the residue, with all the multiplied transactions of a trading country, calls for a liquidator or means of payment, a large portion of these credits will be liquidated by adverse credits and set-offs through the banks of the large cities and centers of trade. The running balance of debt must be paid by the medium until the real credit that was to have canceled it has been found.

To elucidate this position and the mode of canceling debts by the use of credits, I have made the following clearing-house statement of debits and credits, showing how they finally balance each other; a daily repetition of this goes on when trade is brisk.

To receive.	Creditor.		Debtor.	To pay.
....	$500,000	United States	$500,000	....
....	390,000	Europe	400,000	10,000
10,000	210,000	South	200,000	....
10,000	110,000	West	100,000	....
....	90,000	North	100,000	10,000
....	100,000	Other countries	100,000	....
$20,000	$1,400,000		$1,400,000	$20,000

In fact, each city, town, and county clears its own neighborhood and customers. Valuing on the debtors in favor of the creditors to close up, the last debtor will be found to have more goods than he can hold or carry, and must convert in order to get the credits with which to liquidate. I beg a careful study of this table of clearing debts; by its means many intricate positions may be clearly understood,—among others, how fourteen millions of credits will pay fourteen millions of debits, and, above all, how little of *money, gold* or *bank-note* mediums, enters into the daily transactions of great countries, so thoroughly versed in the hunting up of commodities are Europe and the United States. In fact, the amount of gold handled in payment really plays so insignificant a part in the canceling of debt or the purchase of commodities that we are forced to the conclusion that produce alone buys produce and liquidates debt, and that when gold is called for there is no produce, and some one is unable to pay his debt, from a failure chargeable to some account, but not to the circulating account or legal tender. The truth is, this delinquent debtor has nothing to pay for the liquidation and no credit to borrow; he has overtraded or mistaken the market and sold at a loss. The trouble that he is in is not chargeable to the medium or to derangement of its circulation. If legal tenders were as cheap as bankrupt notes, he could not command them. He must stand back and let those come forward who have commodities for exchange; they are able and willing to redeem the medium,—in fact, pay it or convert it into gold or its equivalent.

From the foregoing all unbiased parties can draw the following deduction, which I call a fundamental truth:

If a country require $500,000,000 of a medium and legal tender, and no more than that sum is given them, all surplus of produce and goods and all debts are the basis of the fund in the great banking-house for the redemption on demand which will cause its instant convertibility into gold or any other commodity. No basis of convertibility ever offered by banks of circulation can be as effectual as the conversion in full at all points. I hold, further, that a country giving circulation to its medium, and declaring it a legal tender, will not ask for immediate convertibility into gold, but will trust something to the fortunes of another crop, and to some extent will rely on Providence; but if the promise of convertibility be once found wanting in a mixed currency, all faith is lost, and the determination springs up to realize at once.

This position in regard to the fund held for the redemption and immediate conversion of our inconvertible medium, paradoxical as it may seem, ought to be clearly understood; and, as I claim originality for it (no work I have met with urging this point), I deem it my duty to explain fully the surroundings. In order to do this, I will go to the root of convertibility, and what is to be relied on in the hour of need.

Take the Bank of England. What is the basis of her notes? When issued with fifty per cent. of gold as a basis, all parties know, favorable though this basis may be, that immediate conversion would be an impossibility. It needs no great amount of arithmetical knowledge to see that the half is not equal to the whole. The bank's great reliance is on the ability of the people who are compelled to use a medium. Every man in the kingdom, while the bank is not called on for one dollar of her gold, is converting these notes, daily paying his assets and commodities for them. So long as this is the case, the bank need not fear being called upon for immediate conversion. Now, I hold that the United

States, with her wide-spread territory, offers greater security for the immediate conversion of her notes than can be offered by any other country. The mass of her people have not only a direct interest in upholding these notes, but are compelled to use them in the exchange of her large productions seeking a market. They cannot be much below $2,000,000, which is offered for the redemption of $500,000. If, as the result of a short crop, a sufficient amount is not placed on sale to cover the demands of those who desire immediate conversion, and the tendency should be a decline in value or purchasing power, still the necessity for the liquidation of debt and their use as a legal tender will sustain them until increased production can come to their aid.

Can there be any more effective conversion than the products which man is compelled to have for the supply of his daily wants, coupled with the power and certainty of liquidating debt? Fluctuations and depreciation may occur for a time, but, in the face of the large tax-list, cannot last long. The people will be poor indeed when they have no goods to offer in redemption. If gold be desired by the timid and the speculator, it will still have to be converted into goods to be made useful or productive; if used in the liquidation of debt, it has accomplished nothing more than mess-pork or flour can do.

In a word, all the cotton, mess-pork, and flour in the country is held as the reserve fund to bring immediate conversion, and can be relied on in the payment of any foreign balance; they will do all that gold can do in sustaining credit, besides giving employment to the enterprising trader and building up a virtuous population. Commodities that will bring gold into a country are the equal of gold. After all that can be said in favor of gold, it cannot be commanded if the products offered for it are not more desirable.

There is nothing unnatural in a people undertaking to protect the credit of their country by the redemption or conversion of her notes. It is often done from motives of friendship, where there is no direct interest, even in times of panics. If the correspondent of a well-known house should be forced to the wall, friends will step forward and protest the bills on account of the drawer, often preventing wide-spread disaster. Now that all large commercial cities are connected by telegraph, immediate provision can be made that will be as effectual in payment as if the original payer had honored the drafts.

The same principle would lead the people of this country to come forward and redeem the notes of the government with their commodities and use them in the liquidation of debt. The necessity that compels them to use these notes to-day will, in all likelihood, continue at least while they are prosperous and have commodities to be exchanged.

The disorganizer and speculator for a rise can make a corner in any one commodity, especially gold, if a legal tender, greatly to the detriment of the debtor class, disturbing the relations between all other productions, as well those in second hands as the balance in the hands of the producer. This cannot be the case to any ruinous extent if we have a medium such as has been indicated, with the elasticity to stretch, and which, when redundant, will shrink back into four per cent. bonds, until new products again call it into use. There need be no fear of a protracted redundance of circulation; the exchange of bonds, and *vice versa*, will generally be made in view of a profit. Interest always prompts man to seek the most profitable and safe investments; for this reason, above all others, the medium should be regulated by the parties using it and giving it currency.

A correct appreciation of this principle will explain why any medium has currency. After all, the proportion of gold as a basis, the quick circulator and universal credit, springs from the daily redemption and conversion by the people; they are satisfied with this, and understand its complications. Market reports and quotations of the gold market are not half so tempting as the redemption with pork and flour and the payment of debts. Those who redeem in commodities are not the only ones that show a disposition to sustain the medium. The professional man, the doctor, the lawyer, and the minister, are equally the advocates of a daily conversion.

The indebtedness of a country also gives credit by daily use; but it is the products alone from which final redemption can be hoped for. The two processes, combined, may be likened to Peleg Bissel's churn, which was composed of one big wheel and a smasher. Debt is the big wheel, and commodities are the smasher; one stirs up the fire, the other extinguishes it. Without the big wheel and smasher the Bank of England notes would cease to circulate; there would be no use for a medium if there was no produce to redeem them instantly.

When banks undertake to issue their orders on the people for commodities, their desire to make interest and speculate on credit is carried to such an excess that the people cannot respond. Then they are returned to the owners for payment; and panics ensue, bringing ruin on all traders who may have obligations to pay outside of the banks.

If the people of a country desire gold, the merchant will bring it in return for the exports. It is rarely that the trader neglects the wants of his customers; to do so would be to neglect his own interest. He will bring the gold as willingly as the bread or the calico, if they are able to pay for it. When gold was needed as a medium, money interests were involved, and a great number of parties had to be consulted. From a reduction of the usual bank-note medium and heavy discounts on bills against the exports, the market was frequently over-traded, and then suddenly ran off in the same way.

Allow the producer to order in return for his exports such goods and wares as he may desire, and the market will be as regularly supplied as it is now with calico, tin pans, and pots. If the banker wants gold, let him buy commodities, or bills against them, and import it. Do not force the producer to pay all the charges of bringing it into the country when he may want none of it; his wants may be satisfied with pork, flour, and calico. When the necessaries and conveniences of life are needed, man will export the luxuries and superfluities in exchange for them. Gold being the least useful of all luxuries, it is but natural to send it off first in exchange for the necessaries of existence and reproduction. If the people do not desire gold, and we have our legal tender, they can prevent its import by advancing prices for their productions. This process will establish an equilibrium the world over.

DEDUCTIONS.

1. If the medium and legal tender of a country be merchandise, like gold, desirable for export, it is a curse, in place of a blessing, to the people.

2. All mediums are conventional, and have the value of the goods they will exchange for; legal tenders are made so by law.

3. The true basis of all mediums for conversion is commodities. No proportion of gold to the amount in use is equal to the instant and universal conversion by the people in productions. Couple this with the power of a legal tender, and you have a medium which, if restricted to the wants of a people, will be at all times equal to gold. Bank of England notes, with dollar for dollar as a basis in gold, would not be a reliable or useful medium, if it were not for the tacit promise on the part of

the people to redeem them with the necessaries and conveniences of life. If you convert the medium into gold, these commodities must still be had,— one is as effectual as the other. Commodities, after all, buy each other and liquidate debt.

4. No circulating medium that is not a legal tender should ever be permitted; otherwise, when discredited, it deprives man of the ability to pay debts. How can he pay without products or value?

5. Imports take gold out of the country.

6. If gold is the legal tender, the export articles have all the burden to bear in bringing it back.

7. The amount of tax paid by the exports to keep up a legal tender and sustain bank credits is five per cent. per annum, or $25,000,000.

8. This $25,000,000 is a bounty to foreign manufactories and a discrimination against the home productions by the cheapening of the exchange, and is so much *loss* to the *producer*.

9. Commodities not alongside of each other cannot measure value accurately; they differ in different countries.

10. Gold is not reliable as a comparative measure of value. Its own cost fluctuates; but not so often or so disastrously as the supply at any particular place, causing its value, as a medium or legal tender, to rise or fall.

11. All mediums cost the country the average rate of interest. The lowest estimate on $600,000,000 at six per cent. is $36,000,000.

12. The people that redeem and give currency to the medium should be the recipients of this sum.

13. Bills of exchange, as now used, are the purchasing power and medium between exports and imports.

14. Exports buy and pay for imports, including gold.

15. Balance of trade is the difference between individual speculations, and is a private affair, to be adjusted by the speculators as best they can.

16. Favorable or unfavorable balance of exchange indicates that the banks issuing notes as a medium are being called on for payment. When they pay, the balance will change.

17. Large discounts on bills at an export point are oftener an evidence of prosperity than of poverty; they are an indication of the effort to realize for productions. When gold has to be forwarded to meet the bills, it is an evidence of a scarcity of commodities.

18. The Bank of England remained suspended for nearly twenty-five years; and yet during a portion of that time her notes bore a premium over gold as high as three per cent.

19. Russia issued forty millions of irredeemable notes; they circulated at par with gold for seventeen years, and did not decline until the issues exceeded the demand as a medium.

20. The notes of the Bank of Venice, based on a loan to the government without any promise to pay in gold, commanded a premium over gold of thirty per cent. during nearly five hundred years, and the premium had finally to be restricted by law to twenty per cent.

21. Our present legal-tender medium, if perpetuated and made interchangeable with four per cent. bonds, will adjust itself to the volume of productions with but slight fluctuations from a gold standard.

22. Public debt is based entirely on the surplus productions of the country. No country ever gave its lands and capital stock in payment of debt; to do so would be a surrender of nationality. The principal and interest, therefore, must be drawn from surplus income.

23. When wealth was thought to consist in gold, Europe legislated up to 1663 to prohibit the export and encourage the import. It was *instinct* endeavoring to keep in the country the requisite sum as a medium, in order to prevent undue fluctuations in property that was to be measured by it.

24. The best writers on political economy urge the great expense of gold as a good reason for the many substitutes and devices which man has been compelled to use in the exchange of commodities and the liquidation of debt.

www.ingramcontent.com/pod-product-compliance
Lightning Source LLC
Chambersburg PA
CBHW031816220426
43662CB00007B/667